Sidewalk Contemplatives

Sidewalk Contemplatives

A Spirituality for
Socially Concerned Christians

SUSAN B. ANTHONY

CROSSROAD • NEW YORK

To sidewalk contemplatives
of all times and places,
including my own kin,
who have moved us closer to becoming
a society that renders contemplation
possible for all its members

1987

The Crossroad Publishing Company
370 Lexington Avenue, New York, N.Y. 10017

Printed in the United States of America

Library of Congress Cataloging in Publication Data

Anthony, Susan Brownell, 1916–
Sidewalk contemplatives.

1. Anthony, Susan Brownell, 1916–
2. Catholics—United States—Biography.   3. Women
social reformers—United States—Biography.
4. Spiritual life—Catholic authors.   I. Title.
BX4705.A623A3   1987   282′.092′4   [B]   86–29104
ISBN 0-8245-0795-9 (pbk)

CONTENTS

ACKNOWLEDGMENTS

I am grateful for the valuable help given by the
reference and other librarians at the following: the
Deerfield Beach—Percy White Library; the Main Broward
County Library, Fort Lauderdale; the Florida Atlantic
University Library, Boca Raton; the Saint Vincent de
Paul Seminary Library, Boynton Beach; and to the Social
Issues Resources Series (SIRS), Boca Raton; and to the many
sources quoted in the text and cited in the end notes.

Sidewalk Contemplatives

ONE

CONVERT

One day in 1960 shortly after the breakup of my third marriage, an unheralded sentence floated to the surface of my mind, giving me a wry smile. "If I had spent as much time on God in the past twenty-five years as I had spent on men, I would be a saint."

It is now twenty-six years later. In fact, last year I celebrated the silver anniversary of my life with Jesus. The good news is that the time I have spent on him in the past twenty-six years has led to a radical change in all aspects of my life. He has enabled me to make a breakthrough from my old self, the secular activist-cum-misplaced mystic, to what I call a "socially concerned contemplative." But I have not even come close to achieving the second phrase in that revealing thought: "I would be a saint."

True, like many Christians I "try to try" to be a saint— as I once used to "want to want" to stop drinking when I was an active alcoholic. That I have miles and miles to go to be a saint was shown to me again just five minutes ago. I spoke rudely on the phone to a credit card clerk who was treating me like the dummy I am about figures. Ripped out of sleep far earlier than I liked by my panic over a skin rash, I had already started the day badly. Then this afternoon instead of following the impulse to visit a very sick friend in the hospital, I put it off. By the time I finally called, she told me no visitors were allowed.

1

That redeeming thought, "If I had spent as much time on God in the past twenty-five years as I had on men," had surfaced in 1960 out of the depths of shock at the end of my life as I had known it. I was then married to Jack and living on the island of Jamaica. The thought expressed a goal that would shape my life for the next twenty-six years, up to the moment I sat down to type this manuscript.

Six years earlier survival, not sanctity, had been my goal. Shortly after our wedding in 1954, U.S. security forces, led by the Department of Justice, invaded our plantation and made me a captive of the cold war because I refused to testify in the McCarthy madness. They threatened to invoke Jamaica's extradition-of-witness treaty and have me deported to the United States. Simultaneously, Jack, a Britisher, would be barred from ever entering the United States. Then they denaturalized me, making me probably the first and only American-born citizen in history to be stripped of all citizenship rights.

In 1960, six years after this incident, I flew out of Jamaica, stripped not only of my husband and my nationality but of my property and even the possibility of earning money. It was then that the event occurred that would change my entire life.

It took place on the morning of October 7, 1960, a rainy day thousands of miles from our spice-scented green plantation, in a bleak little brown room at the San Diego YWCA. One second I was standing at the window watching the rain, and the next I was sobbing. I was overwhelmed by sorrow. I was thinking of my mother, of the times during those tenuous first days of sobriety when I had hurt her, cut her bluntly off from me on the grounds that her constant concern might send me back to the bottle. For that long-buried cruelty I suddenly felt contrition—not the remorse of my drinking days when I would be sorry but knew all the while that I would drink again. What I felt was true contrition, a deep, decisive sorrow for having wronged her.

I crossed the room and went to the typewriter. I took off its cover and put the machine on the bed. Then I sat down and wrote a letter to my mother, begging her forgiveness. I typed out the envelope and placed the letter in it. And as I sealed it, the forgiveness came. I knew I was forgiven. I knew that I was forgiven by my mother. As I sat there, I was forgiven by another person, the person of Jesus Christ. In that split and blinding second, I knew that Jesus was not just man, he was God. I stood up, trembling and confused. I went to the window. I turned. And he was there:

"I am God. Before Abraham was, I am."

He held out his arms, "Come unto me, and I will give you rest."

I answered as I surrendered to him, "Yes, Lord, yes."

The greatest of all experiences had happened to me. And it had happened so simply.

I asked him: "Lord, what will you have me do?"[1]

He answered by providing me with an immediate place to stay and with food; he even helped assuage my homesickness for Jamaica's beautiful beaches. He gave me a beach at La Jolla, California, where I could walk and pray while gazing at the Pacific studded with whales' spume and at the seal-like surfers silhouetted against the sunset. The only thing he couldn't provide me with was a paid job. The U.S. Immigration Service had issued me only a visitor's visa. I took advantage of my unemployment to write a piece, "Jamaica Journey," and to learn the contents of my newly bought *Book of Common Prayer*, and to begin reading the Bible. Soon I was invited to stay at the Royal Road health resort in Nogales, Arizona, in exchange for a daily lecture to the guests (when there were any) and for helping out with publicity.

My sun-filled room overlooked the Mexican hills and the red-tiled roof of a church in town. I took long meditation walks out to an arroyo far from the hotel but still on the huge ranch. In the silence and the solitude of the desert I spent many serene hours communing with God. As I prayed, thanking the Lord for his watch over me, I could almost forget my problems with Immigration. However, anxiety over my legal status was seldom far from my mind, and I beseeched God continually for a solution to my problem.

His answer came through one of the resort's visiting speakers, Mme. Induk Pahk, a merry, holy missionary from South Korea. She became a kind of St. Raphael, guiding me to a possible resolution of my predicament. She had been granted permanent resident status through a private bill introduced in Congress. She suggested that I ask my congressman to introduce a similar bill to renationalize me. After praying with her, I wrote to my hometown congressman, Francis "Tad" Walter, who happened to be head of the immigration subcommittee of the House of Representatives (and a friend of my father). My plea for help was answered with an invasion of my Garden of Eden by a posse of immigration officials from the local, state, regional and even Federal level. They interrogated me for hours at a time at the local immigration office. I usually had breakfast and rode down with immigration officials. They always stayed at the Royal Road, along with the local FBI agent, who, by an odd coincidence, had a room near mine.

After months of hearings the regional director of Immigration flew in from El Paso. He placed in my hand the U.S. government's order to deport me from the United States immediately, making official my status as the first native-born U.S. citizen to be denaturalized. I was an alien in my own land. The only thing that saved me from immediate deportation was the intervention of Congressman Walter. He had answered my letter, enclosing a printed copy of the private bill he himself had introduced in the House of Representatives on my behalf. It would, if passed, restore me to my birthright citizenship.

At the same time, there was another event that softened the blow of being legally stripped of my United States citizenship. I was granted citizenship in the kingdom of God on earth—the church. The red-tile-roofed Sacred Heart Church had led me to go down and look inside, then to ask question of Father Theodore Radtke, the pastor, and finally to take instuctions.

On July 30, 1961, I was received into the Roman Catholic church. Two months later I was catapulted from the Royal Road hotel to the only Catholic graduate school of theology in the United States that admitted women, Saint Mary's, Notre Dame, Indiana. Making my admission possible was Father Louis J. Putz, C.S.C., father of the lay apostle movement in the Roman Catholic church, who waved his wand at Saint Mary's and not only got me admitted there but found me a job that would support my graduate studies. In my first months there I felt like a misplaced Auntie Mame, as I, the once fast-track alcoholic, divorcée, deportee, settled into a spiritual discipline of liturgy, prayer, study and work at least as rigorous as that of the nuns with whom I lived.

Four years later, in 1965, I became one of the first fifteen Roman Catholic laywomen in the United States to receive a doctorate in theology (as distinct from religious education).

My doctoral dissertation, entitled *The Prayer Supported Apostle,* was published even before I obtained my doctorate and became the text for both the first national prayer group conference in the Roman Catholic church and the first course on prayer offered for credit in a graduate school.[2] I taught priests, nuns, and lay persons in July 1965, continued teaching prayer for the next nine years, and remain a retreat director to this day.

Our first spontaneous prayer group conference drew 700 men and women to Saint Mary's. It was the seed bed of the Catholic charismatic movement as well as a spur to building conventional prayer groups throughout the country. In 1969 and 1970 the charismatic conferences drew 30,000 praying men and women to Notre Dame (this was part of the international charismatic prayer group movement that would peak at a million members in the 1970s).

I had first found my "place of prayer—a precious habitation," as John Woolman, an eighteenth-century American Quaker, called it, many years earlier while snorkeling in the turquoise water off the Florida Keys. It had crossed those waters to our hilltop farm in the Jamaican forest, flourished in the desert of Arizona on El Camino Real, and hardily survived a transplant to the cold winds of northern Indiana. I had found a place of prayer even in South Bend winters, a beautiful forest with tall trees lining what was once a bridle path. I rushed there during the short lunch period between my double shift as theology graduate student in the morning and as dean of nursing students in the afternoon and evening. In my place of prayer I walked in the stillness of the forest, praising my Lord who had given me this new life in my middle age.

On our second anniversary together my Lord had also given me the gift of contemplation. It first came in the stillness—wordlessly. Then it took form in prayer poems, little verses that gave a "local habitation and a name" in love songs to him, and came from a center in me I had never known existed.

Accompanying that gift was a nearly constant sense of his presence. We were never far from each other those first five years. My entire life was with him—from the prayers written to him, to the early-morning Mass, through my classes in theology and philosophy on the beautiful campus of Saint Mary's and the long hours in my office at the nursing school, where between counseling students and chatting, I managed to type my nearly illegible theology notes before I forgot what had been taught. He armed me to cope with the difficulties, hard work, and cold weather.

His presence also helped me to transcend the bad news a year later of the death of "Tad" Walter, the sponsor of the bill protecting my foothold in America. Because Congressman Walter's bill had died with him, friends introduced me to Congressman John Brademas of South Bend, Indiana. He took up the sponsorship of the bill, calling it "a very difficult case." Though we did not know it, we faced long years of heavy weather in the fight to prevent my deportation, because the new chairman of the House subcommittee on Immigration, Congressman Michael Feighan, was completely hostile to us.

Those years of my captivity in the cold war involved constant rebuff and rejection of my case, frantic calls all over the country, and frequent trips to Washington to throw myself on the mercy of disinterested and often unfriendly congressmen. I spent months writing notes beseeching help—for character references as well as thank yous and requests for prayer. Money was a constant problem for travel, expenses, telephone calls, and huge legal bills I incurred.

My legal status was essentially the same as that of a paroled prisoner. I had to have permission to go even six miles from my dormitory because it was out of the immigration district that served as my "jail," or parole location. I was fingerprinted every time a session of congress adjourned, and of course I couldn't travel outside of the United States. I was warned that I would not be allowed back in.

I could transcend all of this because by some miracle I seemed to be in some kind of spaceship with my Lord, and we floated serenely above my troubles most of the time. I was also fortunate in that I was too involved in school—with papers to write, exams to take, and students to counsel—to have much time for worry. I was not, however, totally immune to the downward pull of gravity, and there were days when I was consumed with fear, frustration, and resentment at being an alien in my own land. I was able to overcome these down periods only by keeping my heart fixed on God.

In addition to my studies, I continued to saturate myself with the lives of the mystics. I had been drawn to them since I had first read Evelyn Underhill's classic book, *Mysticism.* I devoured Sts. Teresa of Avila and John of the Cross. The writings of the mystical saints attracted me far more than St. Thomas Aquinas's *Summa Theologica,* our main theology text in those days. I was particularly impressed by the way in which contemplation was balanced by action in all of them.

During my four years of study I abstained entirely from political action. I was much more immersed in the first century of Jesus than in twentieth-century America. But my political abstinence was more a matter of necessity than choice. As a deportee, immigration officials never let me forget that I could be deported at any time if I became politically active, unless, they said, it was in support of a government action, such as the war in Vietnam.

This restriction on my political activity was not as onerous as it might have been because in spite of the turmoil of the sixties, news seldom reached me. I read no newspapers and listened to no television news coverage, except when President Kennedy was assassinated, and the civil rights struggle was at its height. But remaining so removed from a human community of which I was a part soon proved a heavy cross to bear. One day as my classmates and I convened in the little prayer group we had formed, we prayed for an end to the oppression of blacks, and of the violence being used against them and their white supporters in Alabama at that very moment. We then took up a small collection to send a Dominican classmate, Sister Catherine, to Selma. She went, standing and praying for hours with cold feet and aching back along with thousands of others. She stood up to be counted amid blacks and whites, the police and their dogs. She was representing all of us. I was overcome by a desperate desire to join my sisters and brothers.

In remaining silent I was going counter to a conscience that had been formed by generations of Anthonys who had fought for emancipation and the vote for black women as well as men. Aunt Susan was inspired to join the abolitionist cause when she met the great black leader Frederick Douglass at her father's table. She became an abolitionist, and for the next fifteen years worked in William Lloyd Garrison's Antislavery Society. Not only had her father and other radical Quakers supported Rochester's underground railroad, but Susan's younger brother, Jacob Merritt Anthony, my grandfather, had fought at Osawatomie with the martyred guerrilla leader John Brown against the extension of slavery. It was only by chance that he missed being at Harpers Ferry to hang alongside of John Brown.

It not only stung my inherited conscience but my newly formed Christian conscience to remain outside of the nonviolent struggle for black equality in my own century. But the price of instant and permanent deportation was more than I could pay at that time.

Despite my political abstinence, the U.S. government did not loosen the chains of my captivity. In fact, I was still under the ban in 1967. Now an assistant professor of theology at Marymount College in Boca Raton, Florida, I was sitting at my typewriter one day rejoicing that I had the whole summer free and might be able to finish a book on which I was working when the phone rang. It was Washington calling—the assistant to Congressman Brademas was on the line. Her voice was high-pitched as she said, "Dr. Anthony, are you sitting down? I am afraid I have bad news for you. The committee has killed your bill! You will be deported from the United States in less than thirty days!"

They gave no reason, she had said. They didn't have to. The killing of the bill meant that I had to get ready to leave America immediately, never to return! Congress would do nothing for me. I must report immediately to the immigration director in Miami, she said.

Though numb with shock, I automatically shifted gears into my emergency survival procedure. First I typed a prayer for help, which then became a list of what I needed to do in order to survive, beginning with my call to the immigration director in Miami. Then I made a cup of coffee to remind myself to stay away from a drink should the temptation, born of desperation, become too great. Later I forced myself to eat, even when the immigration director coldly dismissed my plea for an extension of time.

Two days later I was sliding into despair. Then I called for legal help. I got it from an enthusiastic, brilliant southerner in West Palm Beach, Grover Cleveland Herring. He teamed up with Cody Fowler, former president of the American Bar Association, and his Miami partner Walter Humke.

Two years later we had exhausted all legal means right up to the court of last resort, the U.S. Board of Immigration Appeals. The story broke nationally on Good Friday, 1969 that I risked instant deportation. There was a flood of loving calls, wires, letters, offers of advice, and prayer from friends around the nation. What could they do to help? each asked. My lawyers said they could do nothing practical. Even the slightest hint of political pressure on the Board would damage my case.

During prayer on Easter Monday, God gave me an idea. Why not ask all of these wonderful friends who had offered their help to *pray?* If we could not apply pressure here on earth, we could apply it in the spiritual realm where the real battles are fought against the "principalities and powers." Everything else had failed; why not try prayer? Catherine Marshall, the author, and my spiritual director, Father Putz, sponsored a prayer vigil on May 2, 1969. They headed a network of at least 5,000 prayer partners across the nation who conducted prayer services and meetings in churches and cathedrals, on campuses, in convents and monasteries, and even in a federal penitentiary.

On June 26, 1969 at 12:01 in the afternoon I got a phone call from my lawyer's secretary, May Hart.

"You have won," she said. "The board has upheld you. They say that you never lost your citizenship—you are an American. All deportation proceedings have been dropped, terminated, finished. You are free!"

A national prayer action accomplished in eight weeks what eighteen years of hard work had not been able to achieve. All I could do was offer in prayer the old hymn "Now Thank We All Our God" and type it on thank you notes that would be sent to the hundreds of people who had led prayer actions for my renationalization.

I rode the heights of the earth for the next twelve hours. First I called Mother and the family, and then the many helpers whose prayers had set the captive free.

The implications of the victory began to hit me the next day. What Gandhi had said proved true: "Prayer, properly understood and applied . . . is the most potent instrument of action."

My friend Barney Lenahan, however, warned even while congratulating me: "Now, Susan, you got to get used to freedom all over again. Remember, you're just like a prisoner who has been sprung after a long time inside."

He was right. I soon learned that my captivity in the cold war had paralyzed one whole half of my nature, the political animal in me. During my long political paralysis God had activated my contemplative faculties, giving me some clarity on the end and means of human life, as it is ordered to him. And the end, or goal, of human life is, of course, union with God and with our brothers and sisters.

I knew that 1969 was the year I should dedicate as "the year of the Lord's favor" (Isa. 61:2). But how? I had no impulse to run out and use my newfound freedom as a political activist, other than to prepare to vote for the first time since 1952! In fact, it would be several years before I would return to active political involvement. I had spent eighteen years as a captive of the cold war. During the last nine of those years, Jesus had made my yoke easy and my burden light. I wanted first to devote my time to thanking him, which meant that I had first to tell "the glad news of deliverance in the great congregation" (Ps. 40:9).

With a small loan from Father Putz and an advance from a new Christian publisher called Chosen Books, I sat down to the happiest creative year of my life—a year in which God permitted me to write full time without having to support my writing with another job. Though I lived on an unbelievably small income, I prayed and wrote, enjoying what Evelyn Underhill calls "the high spirits peculiar to high spirituality." *The Ghost in My Life* was published in 1971 to the accompaniment of a great deal of publicity—including articles in *The New York Times*, the Washington *Post*, and a number of TV interviews. I survived a grueling cross-country promotional tour in which I made ninety appearances in ninety days from September through early January 1972.

When the transcontinental junket ended I sat down and put on paper my next book, *Survival Kit*, the essence not only of my own survival tools but those of many others. (It was published first by New American Library in 1972 and in a revised second edition by CompCare in 1981.) I enjoyed my firsthand field trips reporting the "green shoots under the nuclear mushroom" sprouting from the new religious left in 1972—among them the ecumenical Center for Dialogue in Miami and the twenty-year-old Catholic Worker movement in the nation.

I was not moved to reenter the secular political fray. Instead I was eager to do what I had dreamed of doing for so long: I founded Socially Concerned Contemplatives (SCC) as an association for the purpose of prayer and action; its first meeting was held in January 1973. Although SCC is nondenominational, its objective was best expressed by Pope John XXIII when he prayed in convoking Vatican II: "Renew Thy wonders in this our day as by a new Pentecost. Grant to Thy Church that, being of one mind and steadfast in prayer. . . , it may advance the reign of our Divine Savior, the reign of truth and justice, the reign of love and peace."[3]

Rooted in Scripture and tradition, the prayer of SCC is both prophetic and personal, putting praise of God for his own sake first but never allowing "hymns to drown out the cries of the oppressed," as Abraham Heschel wrote in his work *The Prophets*.

A gift trip to Europe in 1972 on my restored U.S. passport (confiscated since 1955) led to another spiritual milestone. The trip, though taken partly to promote the English edition of *The Ghost in My Life*, was transformed into a pilgrimage—a pilgrimage to and in Rome. I stayed at the order of the Cenacle Sisters. My guide was an Italian-speaking Cenacle sister. This trip contrasted radically with my college graduation tour of Europe in 1938. Then I had spent most of the time saturating myself with men and booze. In 1972 I saturated myself in adoration and awe of my Lord.

I returned home so filled with fervor that I asked Father Putz if he would approve and receive my taking private vows of poverty, chastity, and obedience. I had been chaste and poor since 1960—chaste voluntarily, poor involuntarily—and now I wanted my material poverty to become a poverty of the spirit as well. I wanted to continue my chastity, and try to try to be obedient to God. Father Putz agreed on condition that I write the vows myself (which I did) and realize that they were noncanonical, i.e., did not require permission from Rome for dispensation, should I ever change my mind. He celebrated my consecration to Christ at a Mass with some of my favorite sisters of the Holy Cross in their chapel at Saint Mary's, Notre Dame, on January 13, 1973.

The Lord seemed to take very literally my vow of poverty. He had freed me from political bondage and restored my citizenship. But now he let me feel the panic of economic bondage. Returning from a month at a house of prayer in the holy land seven months after taking my vows, I discovered that every source of income from lectures, books, and articles had dried up like a cattle pond during a Jamaican drought. Not one penny awaited me or came in after my trip. Even my new manuscript, *Citizen in Your Own Land*, had been rejected. After four lean and frightening months, I took a job as coordinator of substance abuse at the new South Palm Beach County Mental Health Center.

For three years I had enjoyed almost complete control over my time. Now I was forced to conform to the rigid 8:30 to 5:00 regimen of clinic hours. Many evenings I rushed home only to grab a bite to eat and then race back to Delray Beach for an evening meeting. Once a month I was on duty for twenty-four hours in both Delray and West Palm Beach, handling at the latter clinic every single case that showed up on emergency, telephoning the psychiatrist on call (in his comfortable home) for necessary guidance, and putting the nurses on the phone to receive his prescribed medications.

In Delray the poor were served first. I gave most of my time to them, both through counseling the alcoholic poor and founding the first interracial meeting for alcoholics in the area, the black section of Delray. Leaving the shining seaside drive from Deerfield to Delray each morning, at 8:30 A.M. I entered into the stench of fear and poverty that made me call the clinic "ghetto on the gold coast." Spending the bulk of each day with the poor, and feeling poor myself, was not the lighthearted voluntary acceptance of poverty experienced by religious followers who have come from homes of plenty. It was for me a gray reminder of the hard times and depression years of my childhood.

After fourteen years of immersion in religion since my conversion to Jesus, I now felt I was being secularized against my will. I found it necessary to drop his name from my vocabulary. Even the mere reference to a "God of my understanding" in counseling alcoholics or in my therapy groups seemed to give offense. I also had to give up my six years of teaching a daytime class in Scripture and prayer at the South Florida Prayer Community because of my crowded hours. Next my own precious early-morning prayer time was sacrificed to the grind of the clinic hours. Exhausted by work and a low-grade fever, I simply couldn't get up early enough for the extra hour of prayer. Then the walls of the clinic poisoned me. According to my doctor, the formaldehyde lacing the varnish in the flimsy sun-baked structure had given me a serious eye inflammation, breathing problems, and near fainting spells. At night when I fell into my cottage, I was like exhausted workers around the world; I was fit only for sleep or the lull of television.

Countering the absence of private good in my life at this time were two contributions I made to the common good. The first grew out of a therapeutic group I had started at the clinic. I shared with women alcoholics my dream of a rehabilitation center for women who couldn't afford the plush places available in Palm Beach county. The dream materialized as Wayside House, Delray Beach. We celebrated our eleventh anniversary in 1986. As founder and honorary chair, I rejoice that our board of recovered alcoholic women and our director have made Wayside House a nationally recognized model rehabilitaton center for women.

A second contribution to the common good was made through our newly formed Socially Concerned Contemplatives. I called U.S. Senator Harold Hughes in Washington and asked if he would sponsor a bill proclaiming a national day of prayer and fasting. He and Senator Mark Hatfield were successful in getting this bill passed. Churches and prayer groups throughout the country prayed and fasted in penance to cleanse the nation of the corruption in high places revealed by Watergate. We at SCC had already started in common what I had been doing alone since 1969: offering regular prayer on issues of peace and justice.

Now I made a roster of groups that I called "green shoots under the nuclear mushroom," groups that could unite for prayer action on social issues. Until my job at the clinic curtailed most of my extra activities, I shared the message of SCC through national and international prayer workshops, articles, speeches, and prayer conferences.

I had been attracted to the idea of living in community since taking my vows. I looked with longing at the spiritual support and nourishment that living in a religious community could provide. I put out tentative feelers to two or three women to start a residential community of socially concerned contemplatives, but so far nothing had come of it. Finally, late in 1974, exhausted and delayed in the realization of my dream, I substituted a suggestion made by a local pastoral counselor. Instead of trying to establish a community myself, what I should really do, he said, was enter a canonical community, a convent. My own spiritual adviser, Father Putz, expressed gentle but grave reservations about the idea, and I should have listened to him. Instead, I entered the Cenacle convent in September 1975, when I was fifty-nine years old and possibly the oldest living postulant in America.

You can't make a silk purse out of a sow's ear, nor can you make a pliant, virginal nineteen-year-old postulant out of a fifty-nine-year-old divorcée, teacher, former minister, author and prayer-group leader. The novice mistress couldn't have agreed more. She summarily dismissed me in fewer than nine months. I left in tears, with nothing but my private vows, my disciplined prayer life, and friends to sustain me. My poverty now bordered on destitution.

The Lord rescued me through two fortunate happenings. First, I was honored at a huge reception given by the U.S. Senate Subcommittee on Alcoholism for my thirty years of work with women alcoholics. Second, I was asked to appear on a national television quiz show as an expert on women's issues. At the end of five appearances, I had won $16,000.

The massive publicity that surrounded both events launched me on a new career as a transcontinental lecturer at age sixty. From 1976 until 1983 I was queen of the road, flying on the lecture circuit from Maine to Alaska and Nairobi. During those seven years I spoke in all but seven states and traveled almost a million miles. Though my earnings were slim, I was unconsciously following the training I had received as a recovering alcoholic, the gist of which was "keep moving" when in shock. And I was indeed in shock. I had committed my life to the convent and was now being abruptly thrust back into the world. My talks centered on women and alcoholism, prayer and feminism. The flurry over the Susan B. Anthony dollar led to requests for more appearances from the White House on down, miles of copy, and scores of photographs.

In the lively days of the seventies and early eighties, I did not have to muzzle my liberal political opinions. I could speak freely, especially to the Women and Alcoholism movment. I was a delegate to the 15,000 participant National Women's Conference held in Houston in 1977. I also marched in prayer actions with other religious women who joined with secular women at the Seneca Falls Women's Peace Encampment of 1983. We protested the deployment of Pershing and Cruise missiles in Europe. For me, taking part in that nine-hour protest march in the sun and rain was a joyous vindication of the years of burning silence.

I had finally come full circle. I was once more back on the sidewalks of my century, catapulted by the issues of the feminization of poverty, the plight of blacks and the aged, as well as peace. I took part in the twentieth anniversary of Martin Luther King, Jr.'s "I Have a Dream" march, and I have become increasingly involved in the movement for nuclear disarmament.

This has not, however, been a mere rerun of my youthful introduction to the peace movement in the 1930s. My return to the sidewalks of my century during the seventies and eighties has been grounded in a life of contemplation. For the first five years after my stay at the convent, I rented a tiny apartment I called my prayer bower. As I pondered my morning prayer and meditations, then typed my speeches, articles, and books, I looked out upon a grove of royal palm trees. Through their green fronds I glimpsed the white-haired proprietor and his black assistant surveying the condition of the young trees, while a sleek black cat loped like a jungle animal through the dappled sunlight that found its way through the palms. For the past four years the view from my new apartment (also seen from my typewriter) has been two trees grown together—one with golden, the other red, flowers—against a pale turquoise wall. When I turn my typewriter around in the winter, I face the jalousied door to the south, through which I gaze at red and pink hibiscus.

Now my social concern is rooted in the gospel of Jesus and fed by the teachings on peace and justice handed down by the Second Vatican Council and other postconciliar documents (as well as teachings from the Protestant churches), which led toward the official Catholic statement of a "preferential option for the poor," and even to prophetic visions of an economic system that would be an alternative to capitalism. In other words, I am trying to become a sidewalk contemplative, someone who practices prayer and love-in-action in union with God to "advance the reign of our Divine Savior, the reign of truth and justice, the reign of love and peace," a practice that can even lead an individual to "lay down one's life for one's friends" (John 15:13).

In the 1980s we sidewalk contemplatives are no longer alone. We now have companions as well as exemplars in the churches. The work for justice and peace has also crossed national as well as denominational lines. I saw explicit evidence of this in 1984, when I journeyed to the Soviet Union with 265 other peace pilgrims on a trip sponsored by the National Council of Churches. Invited by His Holiness Russion Orthodox Patriarch Pimen of Moscow, we Americans were immersed in the life and liturgy of Soviet believers from Leningrad to Tashkent to Yerevan, Armenia.

The lively spirit of love between the believers of our two nations was manifested in the lines of Soviet churchgoers who cried "*Mir*" (peace) as they greeted us with hugs. We answered "Peace," and returned their hugs. We learned that the place of prayer knows no national boundaries. It is a precious habitation everywhere in the world.

In my own nation I would love to see the spiritual green shoots cooperate with groups working for secular peace and justice in a cultural action—a One Day Buyers' Boycott that might bring about radical reduction in the nuclear arms race and the oppression of the poor. The success of any such action requires disciplined as well as caring sidewalk contemplatives. My own road toward this ultimate goal has followed a path that plummeted to the depths and then soared to unexpected heights. But there is a far better way than the zigzag course I once followed. It is the spiral way to union with God, which in our century has been best explained by Evelyn Underhill. Her classic book, *Mysticism*, describes the perennial philosophy, contemplation, and its spiral stairway—a mysticism not of stagnant isolation but of process, of solidary evolution as well as solitary contemplation.

More than a quarter of a century ago I started to mount the steps of the spiral stairway to union with God, a process I call Breakthrough. Guided by the Spirit, I have tried to do what that redeeming thought suggested to me in 1960—that is, to spend at least as much time on God as I had formerly spent on men. In fact, totting up the time I have spent on God—studying him, teaching him, writing poems to him, and books about him, praying, ministering him through intercession, converting and counseling, leading prayer groups and retreats—would add up to a full-time job, at least over the past twenty-six years.

The quarter century that I have spent on God has helped my new *self* into *becoming* (and even sometimes into *being*). But that is not enough. It is not enough because the new self needs a new *society* in which to survive, to grow, and to flourish—the new society that Jesus came to proclaim. He called the new society the kingdom of God on earth.

St. Thomas Aquinas said the goal of life is "to know the truth about God and live in communities."[4] Aldous Huxley said, "...a society is good to the extent that it renders contemplation possible for its members" and that the "existence of at least a minority of contemplatives is necessary for the well being of any society."[5] But you can only contemplate if you have, at the bare minimum, a vine and a fig tree to sit under, some manna to eat once a day, and peace within and outside your borders.

The Breakthrough steps to the new *self*, first published in my book *The Prayer Supported Apostle*[6] and later in *Survivial Kit*,[7] have helped hundreds of thousands of individuals. I hope that the steps of Breakthrough to a new *society* presented here will serve as a guide to those who are becoming sidewalk contemplatives. We must work with each other to build the new society, the "reign of the Divine Savior," that our new selves need if we are to survive and live as God would like us to live.

The Seven Steps of Breakthrough
from the Old Self in the Old Society
to the New Self in the New Society

1. We admitted that our society has become unmanageable and that

only God can restore us to sanity as we pray: "Thy kingdom come. Thy will be done on earth, as it is in heaven."

2. We sought through prayer, meditation, and contemplation to grow in union with God, seeking his reign within each of us and his reign over our society.

3. We tried to cleanse ourselves and our society of our defects through prayer and purification, and to make amends for our wrongs—personally and socially.

4. We obtained a vision of the best the world could be—the kingdom of God, the new society that God plans for us.

5. We reached a turning point in which the old kingdom of greed battled with the emerging kingdom of God. Resistance to God is stubborn and violent.

6. We surrendered to the reign of God in our lives—personally and socially—practicing obedience to God moment by moment.

7. To get in, and stay in union with God and his kingdom, we practiced these principles personally and in the world around us.

_____ **TWO** _____

BREAKTHROUGH STEP ONE:
ADMISSION AND AWAKENING

Step One: "We admitted that our society has become unmanageable and that only God can restore us to sanity as we pray: 'Thy kingdom come. Thy will be done on earth, as it is in heaven.'"

In the first year of my conversion to Catholicism, 1961 to 1962, I called myself a "rebel in reverse" when I witnessed to my new faith. To me the phrase "rebel in reverse" meant that I was rebelling by becoming a Catholic, rebelling against a long heritage of revolutionary causes that had made me a descendant of dissent. My rebellious ancestors had dissented against the medical profession of London in the seventeenth century. The first Anthonys to reach the colonies (Rhode Island) in 1634 had been religious dissenters and later Quakers. Not only had Grandfather Captain Jacob Merritt Anthony fought as a guerrilla against the extension of slavery to Kansas, but his father, Daniel, had vigorously opposed slavery and raised his daughter Susan B. Anthony to become the "woman who changed the mind of a nation."

When I said I was a rebel in reverse, we Catholics were still in the pre–Vatican II era of Latin and veils. Also, I was in the first flush of my conversion and didn't really know what had hit me. I only began to probe it two years later when I wrote my master's thesis in theology, entitled "The Anatomy of a Conversion."[1] Today as I celebrate my quarter century in the Roman Catholic church, far from claiming to be a rebel in reverse, I rejoice at the connection between the radical social change my ancestors and I sought and the radical personal change wrought in me by my conversion.

Action as well as study has convinced me that conversion, holistically speaking, means personal, social, intellectual and mystical change—and that it is a process, not a one-time happening. I felt blessed that I had not become one of those old-time radicals "who saw the light," "turned" religious, and then spent the rest of their lives retracting, even vehemently attacking, their youthful, radical ideals.

My conversion happily took place on the eve of Vatican II during the reign of good Pope John. The "revolution" already begun in the church by him was far more sweeping than anything I could ever have imagined before I became a Catholic. It was preceded by a revolution in my personal life that began, as it has for so many, by admitting that I had a problem and that I needed help. In fact, I had admitted that I was powerless over alcohol. I had even begun to see that my life was unmanageable.

The truth is that our lives truly are unmanageable. Millions of men and women in our century need a breakthrough from what they are to what they want to be. There are 15 million alcoholics, probably 3 to 5 million drug abusers, and more than 29 million psychologically disturbed or mentally ill persons (mainly outside of institutions). Others suffer from psychogenic but physically manifesting diseases that start them on the road to overmedication of prescription drugs, which in turn sends them to Narcotics Anonymous. Then there are the large numbers who are addicted not to drugs but to work; others are depressed, junkfood gluttons, or spectator-sports addicted. Succumbing to the ubiquitous advertising in our consumer society are the acquisitive ones who "buy more to live more." Finally admitting their financial powerlessness (as creditors close in on them), they join Debtors Anonymous, another of the scores of groups that have copied Alcoholics Anonymous and the twelve steps since its founding in 1935 by Bill Wilson and Dr. Bob Smith.[2]

Bill Wilson hit bottom when there was nothing ahead "but death or madness." All attempts to sober up had failed. He committed himself to Towns Hospital once more and gave up, crying out, "I'll do anything, anything at all!. . . If there be a God, let Him show Himself!"³ Like the prophet who confessed, "I am a man of unclean lips" (Isa. 6:5), there was an immediate response to Bill's plea. His "inaugural vision," which became familiar to the millions who have followed in his footsteps, bears all the marks of a deep religious conversion. Called a "spiritual awakening" in AA today (earlier called a spiritual experience), Bill described his personal breakthrough:

> A wind, not of air, but of spirit . . . blew right through me. Then came the blazing thought 'You are a free man.'. . . I seemed to be possessed by the absolute, and the curious conviction deepened that no matter how wrong things seemed to be, there could be no question of the ultimate rightness of God's universe. For the first time I felt that I really belonged. I knew that I was loved and could love in return. I thanked my God, who had given me a glimpse of His absolute self. Even though a pilgrim upon an uncertain highway, I need be concerned no more, for I had glimpsed the great beyond.⁴

Doubt of the validity of his experience followed this peak even when his doctor, the pioneering alcoholism specialist Dr. William Silkworth, observing Bill, said: "Whatever you've got now, you'd better hold on to. It's so much better than what you had only a couple of hours ago."⁵ Ebby, Bill's friend who had first carried the message of his own sobriety to him, had not had a spiritual experience. But he was guided to bring Bill a book that confirmed the validity of Bill's firsthand religious experience and even clarified it in lucid, limpid, and scholarly language. The book also led in a direct line to Bill's inspiration for Alcoholics Anonymous. It was *The Varieties of Religious Experience* by William James, first published in 1902.⁶

Eagerly reading example after example of spiritual experience chronicled by James in his classic, Bill said later that James, "though long in his grave, had been a founder of Alcoholics Anonymous."⁷

The prestigious Harvard professor of psychology and philosophy concluded in his seminal study of firsthand religious experience of men and women of all and no creeds: "The warring gods and formulas of the various religions do indeed cancel each other, but there is a certain uniform deliverance in which religions all appear to meet." The two parts of this "uniform deliverance" of what he calls "the divided soul" are: "1. An uneasiness; and 2. Its solution."

He then gives the oft-quoted summary of these two parts:

"1. The uneasiness reduced to its simplest terms is a sense that there is *something wrong about us* as we naturally stand.

"2. The solution is a sense that *we are saved from the wrongness* by making proper connection with the higher powers." [8]

The very fact that the individual is aware of his "wrongness" shows that he is ". . . in at least possible touch with something higher, . . . there is thus a better part of him, even though it may be but a most helpless germ. . . . When stage 2 (the stage of solution or salvation) arrives, the man identifies his real being with the germinal higher part of himself. . . ." [9] And the way that one identifies his real being with the germinal higher part of himself, says James, is this: "He becomes conscious that this higher part is conterminous and continuous with a MORE of the same quality, which is operative in the universe outside of him, and which he can keep in working touch with, and in a fashion get on board of and save himself when all his lower being has gone to pieces in the wreck." [10]

How many hundreds of thousands of men and women have been led to admit that they are divided souls, and have awakened to the "germinal higher part" of themselves since James published *Varieties* nearly a century ago? Not only did James help me personally, but his writings plus the miraculous success of the twelve-step program of Alcoholics Anonymous inspired me to create the seven steps of Breakthrough. I based the steps not only on James and AA's twelve steps but on their source in the classical stages of the mystical way that I had first read in Evelyn Underhill's *Mysticism*. This synthesis took place during the summer of 1960 just before my conversion to Jesus as Lord. A few weeks later I consulted Bill Wilson at AA's headquarters in New York. I asked Bill whether he minded if I used the twelve steps of AA as a basis for Breakthrough's seven steps for nonalcoholics. With his long, Lincolnesque face and body he answered warmly, "Susan, the twelve steps are not just for alcoholics —they are for anyone who wants to use them."

Spurred by Bill's permission and encouragement, I began using the seven steps of Breakthrough to the new self in various groups, including prayer groups. They became the basis for my book *Survival Kit* a dozen years later. Still later, the steps took on a life of their own and became the seven steps of Breakthrough to the new society, the basis of this book as printed at the end of Chapter 1.

Here is the relationship between AA's twelve steps, printed below, and the seven steps of Breakthrough to the new self or the new society.

BREAKTHROUGH STEPS	THE TWELVE STEPS OF AA
1. Admission and Awakening	Steps 1, 2, and 12
2. Prayer	Step 11
3. Cleansing	Steps 4 through 10
4. Vision	Steps 4 and 12
5. The Turning Point	Steps 5, 9, 10, 11
6. Surrender	Steps 1, 2, 3, 11
7. Union	Steps 2, 3, 11, 12

Twelve Steps of Alcoholics Anonymous

1. We admitted we were powerless over alcohol—that our lives had become unmanageable.
2. Came to believe that a Power greater than ourselves could restore us to sanity.
3. Made a decision to turn our will and our lives over to the care of God *as we understood Him.*
4. Made a searching and fearless moral inventory of ourselves.
5. Admitted to God, to ourselves and to another human being the exact nature of our wrongs.
6. Were entirely ready to have God remove all these defects of character.

7. Humbly asked Him to remove our shortcomings.
8. Made a list of all persons we had harmed, and became willing to make amends to them all.
9. Made direct amends to such people wherever possible, except when to do so would injure them or others.
10. Continued to take personal inventory and when we were wrong promptly admitted it.
11. Sought through prayer and meditation to improve our conscious contact with God, *as we understood Him*, praying only for knowledge of His will for us and the power to carry that out.
12. Having had a spiritual awakening as the result of these steps, we tried to carry this message to alcoholics, and to practice these principles in all our affairs.[11]

All three sets of steps—for the alcoholic, for the suffering self, and for the suffering society—begin with the admission of one's own powerlessness and the need for awakening to a higher power. It is easier for alcoholics than for sober folks to admit that they are powerless and their lives have become unmanageable. Alcohol abuse is easier to admit than, say, greed. Alcoholism is so antisocial that admitting it becomes a necessity, not a virtue. I speak as an alcoholic as well as a counselor of thousands of alcoholics over the years, in both clinical and private practice. With those suffering from something other than alcoholism, the incentive to admit one's powerlessness is not so great.

Yet two of the most telling texts in the Bible on admission of one's powerlessness and the need for conversion were not directed to alcoholics. One involved the prodigal son, who admitted that his life had become unmanageable. He said, ". . . Father, I have sinned against heaven and before you; I am no longer worthy to be called your son. . . ." (Luke 15:18–19).

St. Paul records another example as he prayed for the thorn in his flesh to leave him. The Lord said to him, "My grace is sufficient for you, for my power is made perfect in weakness." Paul then affirmed, "I will all the more gladly boast of my weaknesses, that the power of Christ may rest upon me. For the sake of Christ, then, I am content with weakness, insults, hardships, persecutions, and calamities; for when I am weak, then I am strong" (2 Cor. 12:7–10).

Though even nonalcoholics may admit that their old *self* has become unmanageable, how can any of us admit that our *society* has become unmanageable and that only God can restore it to sanity as we pray: "Thy kingdom come. Thy will be done on earth, as it is in heaven" (Matt. 6:10)?

We can admit the need for radical *personal* change, but even most Judeo-Christians don't admit the need for radical *social* change, despite the fact that it is spelled out in the Bible by the Hebrew prophets long before the coming of Jesus. They proclaim that changing society is as much a necessity as changing the self. Hear the prophet Amos denouncing the nation of Israel:

"Yahweh says this: 'For the three crimes, the four crimes, of Israel I have made my decree and will not relent: because they have sold the virtuous man for silver and the poor man for a pair of sandals, because they trample on the heads of ordinary people and push the poor out of their path. . . .'" Amos 2:6–7.

And in the fullness of time, when Jesus launched his ministry, he chose as his inaugural sermon the prophet Isaiah's mission for radical social change, not just personal change: "The Spirit of the Lord is upon me, because he has anointed me to preach good news to the poor. He has sent me to proclaim release to the captives and recovering of sight to the blind, to set at liberty those who are oppressed, to proclaim the acceptable year of the Lord" (Luke 4:18–19).

One seldom hears these texts preached from the pulpit. And when we do, too many of us shut our ears and practice denial. One form of denial is what I call the age of anesthesia, a response to the time of trauma in which we live. We anesthetize ourselves with booze, drugs, pills, television, spectator sports, and the greedy grabbing that we call consumerism. We also blot out the vast discrepancy that exists between our way of life and the charter of the kingdom of God that Jesus gave us in the Sermon on the Mount. This discrepancy may appear in the death from hunger and disease (due to

President Reagan's cuts in food and medical care) of children in our own country, or the death, by our bombs, of Libyan children. We can't stand the sight or sound of the instantaneous trauma caused in part by the quakes and shocks of the breakup of the old society.

There is a simple way to find out how aware we are of the gap between the gospel and our society. At the end of this chapter I have suggested "First Tools for Awakening to the Kingdom of God." Tool two directs us to read the charter of the new society: the Sermon on the Mount (Matt. 5–7). (Skip tool three for the moment. It tells you how well you personally live up to this charter on each point of the Sermon.) According to tool four, we should read today's newspaper (preferably the Sunday paper and all of its news section), then grade our society—our nation—on a scale from zero to 100 on how well we live up to the charter, the Sermon on the Mount.

I suggest a Sunday paper because if you are like me, that may be the only day you have time to read the news section thoroughly. When you do read the news section thoroughly, you may, as I do, give very low marks—even flunking our society on how well it conforms to the Sermon on the Mount. By coincidence, Sunday is the day I allow some "poison" for my stomach, while feeding "poison" to my mind. During the week I abstain from such foods as fried sausages, scrambled eggs, croissants, coffee, and marmalade. During the week, I do not spend more than a few minutes listening to the morning dose of news, generally while doing my floor exercises. But on Sunday I let myself go; I allow myself to pore over the paper. By the end of the hour it takes me to do this, I feel as though I have been on a Saturday night binge. I feel angry, restless, gluttonous, and above all frustrated that our society is indeed totally unmanageable, as reflected in almost every news item from terrorism to the continued U.S. attempt to overthrow the legal government of Nicaragua. My gorge also rises at the demolition of any attempts to limit the arms race, Salt II, or others. I then leave for what I hope will be a cleansing liturgy, since I will be reading God's Word from the pulpit as well as receiving and distributing communion. But my yearning to wipe out the bad secular news and replace it with the good news of the kingdom of God on earth is unfulfilled. Seldom do I read aloud prayers of the faithful (already prepared) that even mention the acceleration of poverty or apartheid.

I recently asked a Christian prayer group to grade our society on its conformity to the Sermon on the Mount. I summarized some of the points Jesus made, stressing that the Sermon is addressed not just to *one* person but to *all* the people of his time and ours. In Matthew, chapters five to seven, Jesus promises beatitude—that is, the vision of God—to those who are poor in spirit and humble, those seeking justice, those who are merciful and guileless; those who are peacemakers shall be called children of God, and blessed are those who are persecuted for the sake of justice.

Jesus then defines what should be our relationship with God, with ourselves, and with our neighbors. He commands us to "treat others as you would like them to treat you"—without exception. He told us to turn the other cheek. He told us to love our neighbor as ourselves, and even to "love your enemies and pray for those who persecute you." He urged us to detach ourselves from the love of money, saying, "You cannot serve God and mammon." He assures us that we are to be "perfect just as your heavenly Father is perfect," that is, to follow in his steps.

The members of the group had previously had no hesitation in grading themselves as individuals on the Sermon on the Mount. They were accustomed to the Anglican, Methodist, Presbyterian, and Roman Catholic view of admitting one's personal defects or sins. But out of that group of thirty, only *one* woman even tried to answer the question on how well our *society*—our nation—lives up to the Sermon on the Mount. Amazingly, she said that she thought America lived up to the Sermon *80 percent* of the time, in *80 percent* of its ways. The others did not even bother to answer the question.

Like many Christians, these people were able to admit their need for personal change but not the need for social change. Yes, they would go along with the Beatitudes and the rest of the Sermon on the Mount as a guide to the new self in Christ, but not to the new society, the kingdom of God as Jesus portrayed it. At another meeting, when I mentioned that Luke reported the early church practice and precept "to each according to his need," not each according to his greed (Acts 2:44–45 and 4:34–35), there was a sudden chill in the group. One man said, "That kind of thing just doesn't apply today."

They approved the praying, worshiping aspect of the Apostles shown in the Book of Acts, empowered at Pentecost with the gifts of the Holy Spirit to convert, to heal, to prophesy. But no, they could not approve of the sharing of material goods in the Christian communism of the Apostles. Though the Book of Acts is explicit in its demonstration of a redemptive sharing community in the early church, only small groups of consecrated Christians have infrequently adverted to that goal throughout the centuries. I call them "saints for the common good." By and large, however, the church has until recently conformed to the mores of the dominant elite. Our century, it is true, has seen marvelous changes among Protestants, Catholics, and Jews. But in the prophetic cry for the poor and for peace itself, we remain aliens in our own land—the kingdom of God on earth.

In this age of anesthesia our alienation is implemented by our outright denial of the need for change. It is magnified by nuclear numbing, which has become endemic since Hiroshima. Our awareness is extinguished, and our protest smothered, by deliberate actions of the nuclear war society. The West German theologian Dorothee Soelle writes: "Daily, a little more poison is injected into the minds and hearts of people, a little more conditioning to death. Thinking the unthinkable must be learned."[12] She says that the nuclear arms race is "not a preparation for something that may happen in the future. . . . Rather . . . we prepare for war for so long that it finally strikes as normal. . . . Preparation of nuclear war is the law by which we live. . . ."[13]

She goes on to say that "the threshold of restraint against killing is lowered in anticipation of the future. This creates the present conditions of violence."[14] Soelle then states outright the phrase with which nuclear pacifists and other socially concerned Christians agree:

"Military rearmament dictates social disarmament, as in the United States, where a pre–Franklin Delano Roosevelt state of living outside the protection or the rule of law is being re-established for the underprivileged. . . . Every form of preparation for the military use of atomic power destroys those who are 'preparing.'"[15]

I would add that in my country, the United States, we are already at war—on the poor. And President Reagan is commander in chief of this war on the poor. In fact, his national security state is waging a war of extermination against the poor—denying them food, clothing, shelter, health care, day care, and, for the aged, adequately regulated nursing homes. He is accelerating extermination of the poor on the grounds of both deficit reduction and the nuclear arms race, for which appropriations have soared astronomically through Star Wars.

All the president's men march to the drum of his command and that of the corporate state he rules, staffed by his cronies. His flagrant cuts of life-support services to the poor, made without regard to race, age, sex or color, have already upped, for example, our infant mortality rate. We now rank fifteenth among the other industrialized nations in the preservation of newborn life. These cuts have decreased the resistance of the poor to disease, particularly among children. And they have created a mass of homeless and hungry men and women not seen since the depths of the Great Depression of the thirties. Our tax money is going on guns, not margarine, in the "Reagan Reich."

Millions of Americans read or heard the inscription on the Statue of Liberty during the 1986 centennial. Soloists, such as my sister Charlotte Anthony, sang it at a gala dinner at the July 4 celebration in a New York City restaurant overlooking the tall ships and the fireworks. She and I both wondered how the hungry and homeless of New York felt when they read and heard these blazing words written by Emma Lazarus 100 years ago?[16] What of the mothers with four children in one room, or the unemployed, the forgotten class of the 1980s? How did America's own refugees—the Anglo migrants, and the Mexicans, and other Latins—feel in their fetid rooms when they heard:

Give me your tired, your poor,
Your huddled masses yearning to breathe free,
The wretched refuse of your teeming shore.
Send these, the homeless, tempest-tossed to me—
I lift my lamp beside the golden door![17]

What about those incarcerated by the Immigration and Naturalization Service, refugees from Central America and Haiti who are still locked up at the Krome detention center in Miami, or, even worse, in the isolated "Siberia" camp recently opened in a remote section of rural Louisiana. How do the Arizona church workers and the refugees they helped "illegally" feel as they are convicted, sentenced, and fined for their participation in the Sanctuary movement?

The late R. C. Zaehner, Oxford Professor of Eastern Religions and Ethics, wrote in his Gifford lectures of 1967–1969: "Satan can count as one of his victories . . . the conversion of the American ideal of liberty into the most crassly materialist, soulless civilization the world has ever seen. It is not the Galilean who has conquered but Satan, under whose noonday sun 'we live, and move, and have our being.'"[18]

Strong words, but I believe we must heed them so that we can at least begin to admit that our society has become unmanageable. The good news is that some green shoots under the nuclear mushroom are still sprouting all over the world, even in the United States. Spurred by the impact of Vatican II Documents (still available), Christians are forming more and more green-shoots groups, as we shall see later. And there are still freedoms left, though they are daily diminishing. The CIA recently threatened a major network, NBC, and a major newspaper, the Washington *Post*, with dire punishment should they broadcast or publish allegedly already published news on intelligence operations. And there are print and electronic media that still dare to expose the lies, words, and deeds, committed by the war society, but freedom of speech and assembly have suffered severely. It is no longer safe to hold a small rally (100 to 300) in the city of Miami protesting Reagan's proposed aid to the *contras* in

Nicaragua. But peace and justice meetings are still being held in seminaries, churches and even homes, and they are devoted to praying and sharing on "cultural actions" that might slow down the careening toboggan slide of American democracy into a Fascist state.

One of these actions would be an immediate national day of penance, prayer, and fasting—one bigger and better organized than that led by Socially Concerned Contemplatives in 1973. Our need for penance today is far greater than it was in those days of the unprecedented disgrace of Nixon and his men. Today we need to listen even more to St. Paul, who wrote: "For we are not contending against flesh and blood, but against principalities, against the powers, against the world rulers of this present darkness, against the spiritual hosts of wickedness in the heavenly places" (Eph. 6:12). This would be a national day to unite us in the first step of Breakthrough: "We admitted that our society has become unmanageable and that only God can restore us to sanity as we pray: 'Thy kingdom come. Thy will be done on earth, as it is in heaven.'"

Prayer, fasting, and penance would be the prelude to a further cultural action—one that demands all the time, skill, care, love, and attention that we can muster in the green-shoots organizations as well as the churches. This action would demonstrate the one real collective power we have left—the power to spend or withhold our dollar. I suggest a One Day Buyers' Boycott, carefully prepared through education and organization. It would tell the corporate leaders who are in charge of our nation that we are using the instrument that leaders of nonviolent resistance have often used in their struggles: the boycott. It was effective for Gandhi. It was effective for Martin Luther King, Jr. in the Montgomery boycott. It was effective for President Aquino in the Philippine revolution. And it can be effective for us in the United States today *if* we mobilize the support of the churches, and unions.

A national day of prayer, penance, and fasting would be a day of *admission* that we are wrong as we naturally stand—the entire nation, not just individuals. The One Day Buyers' Boycott would be a day of *awakening* for the dormant mass of Americans who are either anesthetized, alienated, or nuclear numbed. One ounce of action to expose the kingdom of greed and advance the kingdom of God is worth a thousand speeches in waking us up to the truth that we have corrupted our beautiful country and planet—and made our "house of prayer . . . a den of thieves" (Luke 19:46).

Both the day of penance, prayer, and fasting, and the One Day Buyers' Boycott would hasten what the Peruvian father of liberation theology, the Reverend Gustavo Gutierrez, and Paulo Freire call *conscientization*:

> A critical awareness which delves into problems, is open to new ideas, replaces magical explanations with real causes and tends to dialogue . . . the oppressed person perceives and modifies his relationship with the world and other people . . . the oppressed person rejects the oppressive consciousness which dwells in him, becomes aware of his situation, and finds his own language. He becomes, by himself, less dependent and freer, as he commits himself to the transformation and building of society.[19]

It is what the freedom leaders in Latin America have been sharing with the poor and oppressed, thanks to churchmen, philosophers, educators, workers, and unions. Much of the progress that has been made since the Latin American bishops sounded their "preferential option for the poor" at Medellin in 1968 can be traced to the success of *conscientizing* the illiterates while teaching them to read and write, or awakening the literates to their power in prayer and praxis through the ecclesial base communities and worker cooperatives.

Three examples of the results of *conscientization* come to mind immediately. The first is the overthrow by the religious supported Sandinistas of the Somoza dictatorship in 1979. The second is the nonviolent revolution in 1986 led by President Corazon Aquino in the Philippines. A devout Roman Catholic, Mrs. Aquino accomplished this with the backing of her church. They awakened the people to the corrupt Marcos dictatorship. President Aquino's own awakening had been confirmed by the blatant assassination of her husband, once the leading political opponent of Marcos. I would say that President Corazon Aquino is a sidewalk contemplative, for she is not only willing to lay down her life for her friends but also seeking victory of the kingdom of God over the kingdom of greed. This greed was typified by the exposé of the Marcos' reported robbery of billions from the Filipino people (his wife, Imelda, boasted 3,000 pairs of shoes).

Conscientized clergy and laity also played a major role in toppling the lifetime Duvalier dictatorships in Haiti in February 1986. Though they have not changed the fundamental relationship of the classes, both the revolution in the Philippines and Haiti have paved the way for a democratic government. This is particularly true of the Philippines, where even if Marcos's old cronies, the giant growers and corporation heads, do succeed in their already apparent counterrevolution, the Filipinos will have given the world a major example of step one of Breakthrough: "We admitted that our society has become unmanageable and that only God can restore us to sanity...." We have indeed witnessed the miracle that translated prayer power into people power, into a successful nonviolent revolution. In Haiti the transfer of power to the people had not taken place at the time of this writing. But at least the way has been opened by the overthrow of the dictator and his flight into opulent exile with the reported billions he and his father had extracted from the poorest country in the Western Hemisphere.

It is no coincidence that these three poor nations—Nicaragua, Haiti, and the Philippines—had been given some pastoral teachings on the church's "preferential option for the poor." Despite the overthrow of dictatorships in these Third World nations, we in the First World remain anesthetized in our thinking and voting. Whether Catholic or Protestant, it is as if we had never heard Jesus quoting Isaiah the prophet, that we have been anointed to "preach good news to the poor . . . to proclaim the release to the captives . . . to set at liberty those who are oppressed...." (Luke 4:18)

Indeed, the fastest growing Christian sects are the fundamentalists who ignore this teaching. Dorothee Soelle says:

> . . . the so-called electronic church . . . peddles a sentimental, individualistic successful Jesus. This Jesus is not concerned with hunger, racism or militarism. He concentrates on the salvation of your very personal soul. He is tailored to middle-class hopes. He has nothing to say to the poor, to single mothers, to young blacks who must choose between prison and the military. Out of his mouth you hear much about salvation and nothing about justice; his Jewishness has been taken away from him.[20]

Summing up she further says: "I believe that whenever that occurs nowadays we confront a phenomenon which I am inclined to call Christo-fascism. Here the authentic, the Jewish, the poor Jesus, is forgotten and nullified."[21]

Sidewalk contemplative Rabbi Abraham Heschel, author of *The Prophets* and street demonstrator for civil rights, especially at Selma, Alabama, said: "The well being of the world depends upon the presence within the world of unworldly men [and women]." And I would add that the kingdom of God in the world depends upon the presence in the world of men and women like the rabbi and the other sidewalk contemplatives discussed throughout this book. These are the men and women who build upon union with God as the beam of the cross; the arms of the cross form their union with their neighbors.

The entrance antiphon, based on Rev. 5:9–10, for Friday of the fourth week of Lent states: "By your blood, O Lord, you have redeemed us from every tribe and tongue, from every nation and people; you have made us into the kingdom of God." I believe that the kingdom of God will come when we awaken to the person of Jesus Christ and the spiritualization *and* socialization of his gospel in our personal, social, intellectual, and mystical life. But the kingdom will only take root and bear fruit in our lives if we give it away to each and to all, using the fruits of the Spirit to build the kingdom "on earth, as it is in heaven." Only then will not only each but all reap the fruits of the Spirit—love, peace, and joy in a new spiritualized and socialized humanity crowned by union with God and unity with our neighbor. But let us admit as a first step that our society has become unmanageable and that we of ourselves are powerless. It is the Father who does the work.

An old spiritual writer, St. Cajetan, once said, "No one can fall who lies on the ground. And no one can sin so long as he is humble." Let us lie on the ground. Let every knee bow, and every tongue confess that we as a society have failed to live the *whole* gospel of our Lord. Wherever you are, even if you have some of the limitations listed below, you can begin using the tools of Breakthrough, now, today.

1. If you can read, or even if you can't read, but can only listen to tapes.
2. If you can get to a library, or even if you have to have books brought to you.
3. If you have a Bible (it is free).
4. If you are in your right mind or even a little bit out of it, you can seek the kingdom now, viz., L'Arche of Jean Vanier.
5. If you are living in filthy conditions in a migrant camp in Florida.
6. If you are a retiree whose last prospect seems to be death in destitution, or neglect in a nursing home.
7. If you are in jail, or in exile for political reasons.

First Tools for Awakening to the Kingdom of God

1. Ponder

   Step one: We admitted that our society has become unmanageable and that only God can restore us to sanity as we pray: "Thy kingdom come. Thy will be done on earth, as it is in heaven."
2. Read the charter of the new society: The Sermon on the Mount, Matt. 5–7.
3. Grade yourself on a scale from zero to 100 on how well you personally live up to this charter on each point of the Sermon.

4. Read today's newspaper and/or listen to a TV newscast. Grade our society—our nation—on how well *it* lives up to the charter in the Sermon.

5. Recite the Lord's Prayer not only for yourself and your private intentions but for the whole society, the world. Remember, it is *"our* Father," not "my Father."

6. Meditate on the gospel texts on the kingdom, especially Matt. 25:31–40.

THREE

BREAKTHROUGH STEP TWO:
PRAYER

Step Two: We sought through prayer, meditation, and contemplation to grow in union with God, seeking his reign within each of us and his reign over our society.

The term *prayer*, as it is used in this book, is the soul's spontaneous communication with God—private or public, vocal, silent or written.[1] Broadly defined, it is "our whole life toward God," or ". . . the Godward movement of the soul" in response to "grace, the manward movement of God's love." "*Lex orandi est lex credendi.*" The standard of prayer is the standard of belief. Ask believers, "Where are you in your prayer life?" Their answer generally tells you the condition of their personal spiritual life, their entire life of faith. For prayer is the premise for any progress in one's personal spiritual life, and without it there can be no salvation. Upon our private communication with God depends our entire supernatural life, our whole movement toward God, our life of living faith.

The distinctive note for a Christian, however, is not the goal of personal salvation alone. It is our love-in-action toward our brothers and sisters. Spiritually, we can only keep what we give away. But we can only give away what we have, and what we have depends upon what we have received from God's grace in prayer. The standard of prayer is also the standard of the spiritual life of nations and epochs. Prayer is the only universal language. In prayer the solidarity of the human race in its common creatureliness before the Creator comes forth in the suppliant cry, "Father." As Arnold Toynbee has said, "The Abba Pater, addressed to the Transcendent God, forms the only certain foundation for complete brotherhood among men."²

A praying people of God are a united people of God seeking, in hope, union with God. Prayer hopes for the kingdom of God in heaven and for the restoration of unity, both within the individual and among all persons in the kingdom of God on earth. Those of us who would work for the kingdom of God on this earth must be grounded in prayer for the self and for society. Our model for this is Jesus, a socially concerned contemplative who exemplified the balanced Christian life of contemplation-in-action. He healed, rescued, and taught in the marketplace, but he drew aside to the desert or the mountains to spend time alone, contemplating the Father. Today we socially concerned contemplatives try to emulate Jesus, to lead the two-way life of contemplation and action. We pray for union with God, and we pray and act for union with our neighbors throughout the world, especially the poor.

But Jesus was more than a socially concerned contemplative. His life contains the further note of being a sidewalk contemplative. As defined in chapter one, a sidewalk contemplative is one who practices prayer and love-in-action in union with God to "advance the reign of truth and justice, the reign of love and peace" (Pope John XXIII)—a practice that can lead an individual to become willing to "lay down one's life for one's friends" (John 15:13).

Jesus prayed for the poor, and he prayed for peace, condemning in harsh words and action the profiteers in the temple (Luke 19:45–46; Matt. 21:12–13; Mark 11:15–17; and John 2:14–16). He contrasted God's salvation for the man who humbled himself praying, "God, be merciful to me a sinner," who was rewarded in heaven, with the proud Pharisee who was cast down (Luke 18:9–14). He gave us a gospel of nonviolence in the Sermon on the Mount (Matt. 5:20–26) and a strong injunction against even resentment in Mark 11:25. He was called the Prince of Peace by the prophet Isaiah (9:6).

Jesus said "... seek you first the kingdom of God and his righteousness, and all these things shall be added unto you" (Matt. 6:33). Yet he showed by his nurturing prayer actions that he realized you can't contemplate endlessly if you don't eat. So he fed the multitude (Matt. 15:29–32; Mark 8:1–8; and Luke 9:12–17). He also stressed that you can't contemplate unless you forgive your neighbor (Mark 11:25). Nor can you contemplate if you are in constant fear of the four horsemen of the Apocalypse (Rev. 6:8).

Imitating Jesus, the apostles show in the Book of Acts that they combined contemplation with action—praying, celebrating Eucharist together, then going out on the sidewalks to preach and heal. Like him, they shared what they possessed with the poor. Luke stresses this sharing of goods by writing about it twice in the Book of Acts:

> And all who believed were together and had all things in common; and they sold their possessions and goods and distributed them to all, as any had need (Acts 2:44–45).

Again he writes in Acts 4:32, 34–35:

> Now the company of those who believed were of one heart and soul, and no one said that any of the things which he possessed was his own, but they had everything in common.... There was not a needy person among them, for as many as were possessors of lands or houses sold them, and brought the proceeds of what was sold and laid it at the apostles' feet; and distribution was made to each as any had need.

The Apostles encouraged believers to petition God for answers to both their temporal and spiritual needs. After the descent of the Spirit at Pentecost, they and St. Paul practiced and taught prayer in the Spirit.

The spread of the gospel led not only to Christian communism and the evangelization of the Empire but to death under the Roman sun on the blood-drenched sand of the coliseum and to upside-down crucifixion in the Roman squares or outside the city. One of the martyrs of the postapostolic era, St. Irenaeus (d. A.D. 202), clung to the goal of contemplation until the end, writing: "The glory of God is a living man; and the life of man is the vision of God."[3]

With the Emperor Constantine's conversion to Christianity in A.D. 313, the primacy of prayer and contemplation in the lives of individual Christians suffered a serious setback. The new royal convert immediately made Christianity a status as well as a state religion. Instead of martyrs throwing themselves at the jaws of the lions in the arena, Christians now marched to the drum of upward mobility conferred by their sudden access to the imperial bureaucracy of Constantine the convert. In the wake of this, contemplatives fled the city for their lives—their spiritual lives—taking refuge in the deserts of Sinai, Palestine, and Syria. At first they were hermits like their spiritual father, Antony. But a younger contemporary of Antony, Pachomius, gathered a group of male ascetics into a monastery. He gave them a rule and induced them to live in common discipline under an abbot. The system prospered. Not only were other male monasteries founded, but so were convents for women. Christian communism as well as contemplation found its home in the monastic life that has continued to the present century.

St. Benedict (d. ca. 550) was the first to open the doors of his monastery to everyone, literate or illiterate, at Monte Cassino, Italy. His rule, based upon prayer and work, endures to this day. One of his contributions, revived in the 1970s, was meditation based upon the ceaseless silent saying of "a little verse" of Scripture. He had learned this from John Cassian (d. ca. 435), an Eastern monastic whose conferences on prayer are taught today.

Back on the farm or in the city, however, the ordinary Christian got little in the way of instruction or example in prayer leading to contemplation. Earnest prayer had been replaced by mechanical popular devotions and a formalist liturgy in Latin they could not understand. This naturally widened the separation between the people of God and the Word of God.

Fortunately, some contemplatives remained on the sidewalks to shine not only through the Dark Ages but above the growing corruption of the church. St. Catherine of Siena, doctor of the church

(d. 1380), chose the sidewalks of her city, not a convent, for her prayer actions and converted thousands to a renewed faith. She prayed at home. Then she marched into action at a time when most of the male contemplatives were locked away in their monastic cells praying, translating biblical and classical works, or administering their vast monasteries. Although she was poorly educated, Catherine cajoled, prayed, and threatened the reluctant pope to return to Rome from Avignon, where he had been cowering in exile. Calling her "the mother of a thousand souls," Evelyn Underhill described Catherine as a "great active and a great ecstatic: at once politician, teacher and contemplative."

While some of the earlier monks entered religious life in search of spiritual well-being alone, the new mendicant or begging orders of the thirteenth century were evangelicals—almost sidewalk contemplatives. The greatest of these, of course, was St. Francis of Assisi (d. 1226). In the Golden Age of Mysticism (eleventh through fourteenth century) there are scores of great contemplative-actives who, fortunately for us, have left their thoughts as well as their prayers in writing.

Though it is unlikely that many ordinary Christians spent their days in contemplation, during the first thirteen centuries contemplation was considered a goal for all earnest Christians, the idea being that all prayer should lead to contemplation. But the serpent entered the Garden, separating contemplation from prayer and meditation. The transcendent experience of God began to be replaced by an intellectual probing of theological propositions, or by excessive mortification in which meditating on one's sins took precedence over communing with God. With its emphasis on outer, rather than interior beauty, the Renaissance widened the gap between Christians and contemplation. The majority of believers practiced their devotions, expressed not only in relics and rosaries, but in indulgences, pilgrimages, and church building. But Renaissance popes were distracted by political and economic battles for the survival of the church, and some of them were corrupt.

When Martin Luther, himself a man of deep prayer, struck his blow for the reform of the church in 1517, far from closing the gap between Christians and contemplation, he widened it. Anglican Bishop Kenneth Kirk notes that ". . . the primacy, in private devotion, of worship, contemplation, mystical prayer, the vision of God, . . . was allowed to lapse by Protestantism."[4] From having a uniqueness all its own, prayer became merely an auxiliary effort—a means of securing, or attempting to secure, what lay beyond the immediate reach of unaided will.

A major exception was the founding of the Society of Friends in the seventeenth century. The Quakers, with their silent worship, have become the most enduring and most successful community of sidewalk contemplatives in history. Following the example of their English founder, George Fox, they combined the silence of their meeting with ardent social action for the poor and the oppressed, and for peace. One Quaker, John Woolman, became the father of the abolitionist movement in the American colonies in the eighteenth century. His classic, *Journal*, is a manual for sidewalk contemplatives today.

By the eighteenth century, contemplation had fallen into such ill repute due to the alleged excesses of the Quietists that mere mention of the word was considered grounds for being sent to the Bastille. However, one Jesuit priest, Father Jean-Pierre de Caussade, wrote a book, *Progress in Prayer*, in which he defended the practice of contemplation. Because of the danger of the subject he was forced to publish it under the name of a friend, already an accepted author, whose prestige got the book past the official censors.

In England the solitary star of sidewalk contemplation during the Georgian age was William Blake (1757–1827). Prophet, painter, poet, and visionary, he literally lived on the sidewalks of his century —especially when he was evicted for not paying his rent.

In the nineteenth-century United States, sidewalk contemplatives became leaders in the abolitionist and women's rights movement. Lucretia Mott, the holy Philadelphia Quaker and an ardent abolitionist, helped found the American women's movement in 1840. My great-aunt, Susan B. Anthony, inspired by her Quaker father, Daniel, and his Quaker heritage, joined Lucretia and Elizabeth Cady

Stanton in the women's movement in 1851 and became the most active abolitionist of the trio, working full time for William Lloyd Garrison's Antislavery Society in New York State as well as in the cause of women's rights.

In our century, sidewalk contemplation has taken a giant leap forward through Dorothy Day, cofounder of the Catholic Worker movement. She carried contemplation to the sidewalks of New York's Lower East Side. She not only served the poor but lived with them, voluntarily sharing their poverty. She is, I believe, *the* saint for our century.

The convert Thomas Merton—Trappist monk, poet, contemplative—returned to the sidewalks of his century via his militant columns, which he wrote for Dorothy's penny-an-issue paper, the *Catholic Worker*, as well as his books and articles on peace and justice.

A giant among this century's sidewalk contemplatives was Mahatma Gandhi, the Hindu ascetic and mystic. He daily combined prayer and fasting with massive prayer meetings and the most effective cultural actions in history. He led the teeming millions of India to take not only to the streets but to the river, the sea, and to the ultimate risk. His leadership resulted in a successful nonviolent revolution, one made violent by his assassin.

Evelyn Underhill, the Anglican scholar-contemplative-retreat director, and author of the perennial bestseller *Mysticism*, wrote of the need for the socialization as well as the spiritualization of society.

Dag Hammarskjold, secretary general of the United Nations, proved in his posthumously published book of mystical verse, *Markings*, that the spirit can break through even to one who carries the world on his shoulders. Hammarskjold ultimately gave his life while peacemaking.

Pierre Teilhard de Chardin, Jesuit priest, paleontologist, and poet, was forbidden to teach at the University of Paris and exiled to China because of his evolutionary writings, particularly his masterpiece, *The Phenomenon of Man*. A mystic as well as a scientist, Teilhard expressed deep concern for the world and its future. Fortunately for the future of the earth, as well as the future of the church, one of his admirers was the priest who was to become Pope John XXIII. The influence of Teilhard's writings permeates John's encyclicals— *Mater et Magister, Pacem in Terris,* and the documents of the Second Vatican Council, especially "The Church in the Modern World."

These men and women who have kept the vision of God—the practice of contemplation—alive through the centuries realized that God is indeed the country of the soul and that it is possible to live in that country, wholly identified with it, and still keep one's personality intact. These saints, mystics, and contemplatives have been the artists of eternal life. Yet they have lived in the same nations and toiled in the same tasks as you and I. Their reports on the country of God are not reports of esoteric, exotic experiences. They are reports of what should be our native land, the kingdom of God on earth.

Despite the example of these spiritual giants throughout the ages, prejudice against contemplation still remains. "We have changed our tactics, but the battle goes on. We no longer scorn the mystics; we exalt them above all measure—supermen [and women] who have almost nothing in common with us."[5] Fear of the very word *contemplation* is almost as great as prejudice of the word *mysticism.* As a result, most Christians do not even pray that God lead them to the goal of union through knowledge and love, let alone presume that it is the normal term of the prayer-supported life, here and now.

The tragedy of this separation of the people of God from the vision of God is first that as members of the human race we are failing to fulfill the plan of God for his kingdom. By not even trying to advance to the unitive state, we are failing to become the saints he wants us to be. In other words, we are not even trying to "be perfect, as your heavenly Father is perfect" (Matt. 5:48).

As individuals, the tragedy is even more poignant. "For Thou hast made us for Thyself and our hearts are restless till they rest in Thee," St. Augustine wrote 1,500 years ago. The extent of our restlessness is revealed in the statistics on physical and mental illness. We try to mend the breach in our divided souls with the anesthesias of alcohol, drugs, casual sexual relationships, mindless entertainment, and ultimately violence.

Though made for God, human beings have made for themselves a thousand synthetic substitutes to sate their thirst. Part of the blame for this distortion can be placed on the fallen nature of humanity itself; part of it on the structure of the world we have devised. Not blameless, though, are those who failed to put first things first—that is, the attainment of union with God through knowledge and love in prayer.

If even a few thousand Christians—priests, ministers, religious and laymen and women could be imbued with the mission to restore the vision of God to the people of God, a transformation could occur. However, we will never be able to restore the vision of God to the people of God unless we ourselves have experienced it. People are only partly convinced of the possibility of contemplation for themselves when spiritual writers are quoted. What really convinces them is the witness of those of us who have experienced contemplation. When I witness to the fact that I was a pagan in belief and practice for many years but through the grace of God and prayer the gift of contemplation came to me, they often say, "If you can do it, so can I."

Like most people, I began my prayer life with petition. Petition is the most basic form of prayer, but it is certainly never to be denigrated or abandoned. We will be petitioning for "becoming things of God" until the day we die. Yet I find that there are still many Christians who feel guilty about praying for their own temporal needs and those of their friends. Petition is based on the creature's dependence upon his Creator. It could never have been ignored if the people of God had remained in close touch with the Word of God. Even a brief glance at the Old Testament shows that God was extremely personal to the Israelites and that there was a constant dialogue in man's plea to God and God's answer to man.

Certainly this dialogue continues in the New Testament. In the Lord's Prayer Jesus himself instructed us to pray for our temporal needs, to petition God for our daily bread, and to deliver us from evil in this life. Paul instructs believers to make *all* their requests known to God in prayer, and James says we are to ask for God's wisdom in making the decisions that confront us every day. James also says that we should ask God for physical healing. Clearly the Apostles and the writers of the New Testament saw nothing wrong with asking God to meet our temporal needs.

St. Thomas agreed, quoting St. Augustine's dictum that "It is lawful to pray for what it is lawful to desire." St. Thomas further defended the prayer of petition, saying that we don't pray in order to make known our desires to God, but to remind *ourselves* of our dependence on God. "He wishes to bestow certain things on us at our asking . . . that we may acquire confidence in having recourse to God and that we may recognize in Him the Author of our goods."[6]

The church has never completely lost sight of the importance of petition, and in most church services today—Protestant or Catholic —time is set aside for the formal "prayer of the faithful." Petition by itself, however, is not enough. Petition is still the most of me and least of God. Although petitions for justice and peace are preferable to praying for a new car or a computer, a shopping list is still a shopping list. While God is pleased to meet our needs, he desires more from us and more *for* us. He desires nothing less than union.

Meditation has traditionally been viewed as a bridge between the prayer of petition and the practice of contemplation. It has many definitions, one of which is simply "pondering with assent."

The Psalms are a handbook of meditation as well as petition. Meditation is used to describe the heart, the dwelling on the law and on the love of God. In the New Testament our Lord retired to the mountain to meditate (Luke 9:18). Mary is recorded on several occasions "storing" the Word of God "in her heart" (Luke 2:51). Her Magnificat (Luke 1:46–55) is one of the most beautiful meditations in Scripture. (It is also an excellent anthem for sidewalk contemplatives, especially verses 51–53.)

The subject of my first meditations was not God but mortals, movie stars, and characters in novels. Later, in my teens and twenties, my meditations centered on the boys and men in my life. From morning until night, like most American girls, my thoughts were consumed by the object of my attention. He, for that month at least, determined my diet, the cut of my coiffure and clothes, the tone of my voice, the flippancy or sobriety of my manner.

Meditation on mortals finally gave way to meditation on truth and beauty. Then slowly, oh so slowly, on God. After I finally met Jesus, my meditations centered on him and his Word. I memorized his words and even carried little notebooks with me so that if a word or phrase came to me in silent meditation, I could write it down to keep.

In the twenty-six years since my conversion to Jesus I have practiced and taught many forms of prayer and meditation. For the most part meditation was called "discursive"—that is, using the rational mind, whether in silence, stillness, or writing. St. Ignatius of Loyola was one of the great teachers of this school. He suggested using reason and the senses to imagine pictures of Jesus, a scene from the gospel—the sounds, sights, smells, and taste. But I was drawn over and over again to a different kind of meditation, one for which I had no name. Between classes and work, or later after work at night, I would walk in the forest at South Bend or by the sea at Deerfield Beach, meditating on a single verse of Scripture, or the Jesus Prayer, a single quality that the Savior showed in his life. I didn't realize I was practicing *lectio divina*, pondering the Divine Word. Nor did I know until later that I had been drawn back to the early Christian form of meditation that leads one into contemplation. It was no longer I who meditated, it was God who prayed in me. I was gazing at him with the eyes of ardent love. In other words, I was *contemplating* him.

I began to meet others who had received this gift from the Lord, and my awareness was heightened by reading and listening to the tapes of Dom John Main, the Irish Benedictine. He retrieved the fifth-century conferences on the Christian contemplation of John Cassian, adopted by St. Benedict in the sixth century. Father Main called this unceasing repetition of a prayer word or mantra Christian meditation. He founded a center for its practice and dissemination at Ealing Abbey in London, followed, in 1977, by the Center and Benedictine Priory in Montreal.

Stimulated by Father Main's books, including the recently published *Letters from the Heart*, and scores of tapes, the center has spawned hundreds of meditation groups throughout the world.[7] I had the great joy of making a retreat at the Montreal Priory with Dom Laurence Freeman, spiritual successor and prior since Father Main's death in 1982. I spent six days in the silence, with three periods of half-hour each in meditation daily, following our reading of the Office with the Benedictine community.

Back home I followed the twice-daily discipline of the mantra suggested by Father Main: "Marantha!" (Come, Lord Jesus!) (Rev. 22:20). I find it easier to repeat the mantra early in the morning for twenty-five minutes than to do so before dinner. But I try to persevere. As directed, I sit with straight spine in the stillness and silence of my little apartment. Eight months after I began saying the mantra daily, I rejoiced in the start of the first Palm Beach County meditation group, which has met every Thursday evening since February 1986. Meditation groups are flourishing from Montreal to Australia and New Zealand, Africa, and of course the United States and Canada. Father Main's teaching has even reached into the Bible belt at Mars Hill College (Baptist), North Carolina, as we shall see later.

When Dom Laurence Freeman visited Florida in 1986, I interviewed him on Christian meditation. This is what he said:

> People often ask, Why should I say the mantra the whole way through the meditation? The oldest Christian tradition of the mantra teaches the continuous repetition of your prayer-word from the beginning to the end. This is the key to understanding the absolute simplicity of meditation. Simple, though not easy!
>
> As Christians, we say the mantra in response to Jesus' summons to leave self behind. What this means is something so radical and yet so simple—childlike is how Jesus described it.

Put briefly, it means that we stop thinking about ourselves. We stop *thinking*, as such, altogether. We enter into the greater consciousness of prayer—the mind of Christ—which is a purely loving state, quite unself-centered.

The Christian meditates as a discipline—as a disciple—not as a technique. Said continuously the mantra is a discipline. Saying it as a way to bring about a certain desired state is to reduce it—and prayer—to a technique. The state of prayer is unself-conscious. We should not be analyzing ourselves, our experience, or trying to create any kind of experience. No part of our consciousness should be observing what is happening . The kingdom of heaven does not admit of observation. You cannot say, Look, here it is or there it is. Jesus also said 'set your mind on the kingdom before everything else.'

It may take you a long time to be able to say the mantra continuously. It is not easy to unhook ourselves from our egoism. But even as we learn, we grow in other centeredness, and the sign of growth will be an increase in love. Wholeheartedness, undivided consciousness, total simplicity in, or an absolute response to, the absolute generosity of God. If you can understand these as the conditions of prayer, you will understand why we are meant to say the mantra continuously. It allows us to make the total gift of self that completes the cycle of love begun at our creation.[8]

Meanwhile, the centering prayer movement, another contemplative renewal, draws participants through its active teachers and authors, Abbot Thomas Keating and Father Basil Pennington, both Cistercians. Based on the fourteenth-century Christian classic *The Cloud of Unknowing*, centering prayer groups and retreatants pray in stillness and silence.

The increasing numbers of ordinary Christians in prayer and meditation groups today are proof that contemplation is not a stage of prayer reserved only for the perfect. It is the end and goal of all prayer. I compare our growth toward contemplation with the development of a professional violinist. She perfects her playing until she gains technical proficiency from her discipline. But she is still playing with a certain self-conscious attention to technique. Suddenly one day, if she is faithful to her muse, the music begins to play *through* her. Then she becomes a virtuoso.

So it is with contemplation. We plod along with our daily petitions and discipline of meditation. Then one day, whether we are seated in a quiet room or strolling along the bank of a gently flowing river, something happens. Suddenly our prayers come from a mind other than our own, or even from another heart. We get a glimpse of God such as we did not know existed, but we do know that the glimpse did not come from our discursive mind. It was given. It is not attained directly by mental effort but only by fidelity to prayer, to listening, more than to talking or even writing.

Fortunately God does not limit himself to beautiful places and peaceful days. God is everywhere, even as you look over your typewriter at the brick wall a few yards away or stand in a grimy subway station at rush hour. In his litte book, *The Practice of the Presence of God*, Brother Lawrence reminds us that God is also very much in the clutter of pots and pans and the noise of the kitchen.

The French philosopher Jacques Maritain and his wife Raissa taught that "contemplation . . . depends essentially on the gifts of the Holy Spirit . . . [It] . . . is thus the domain of the liberty of the Spirit who breathes where He wills and no man knows whence He comes or whither He goes. [Contemplation] implies that the soul . . . submits with docility to the Spirit's guidance. . . . Contemplation is the fruit of the indwelling of the Blessed Trinity in the soul and of the invisible mission of the Son and the Holy Spirit."[9]

Pope John's prayer to the Holy Spirit for a "new Pentecost" seemed to have its first answer even before the contemplative revival of the seventies got fully under way. The charismatic renewal began in the Episcopal church in the 1950s and reached the Roman Catholic church in 1967.

The Book of Acts became the handbook of this growing number of charismatics. They believed they would receive power when the Holy Spirit came upon them—and they did. They received power to prophesy, to pray in tongues, to be a channel for healing, and sometimes, when the other conditions were fulfilled, they received the gift of contemplation.

The charismatics made great strides in self-oriented prayer, stressing their intimate relationship to God. Unfortunately, they did not heed the second goal of Pope John's prayer for society, "to advance the reign of the Divine Savior, the reign of truth and justice, the reign of love and peace." Nor, with the exception of Socially Concerned Contemplatives, did they draw many of the green-shoots groups (I formed and continue to form a kind of bridge between the religious left and religious center, as well as between the religious and secular left).

The charismatics brought about a much needed renewal of interest in Scripture, but they focused mainly on those scriptural passages that deal with the individual's relation to God. They ignored the passages that deal with peace and justice, and distanced themselves from the church's preferential option for the poor. They continue to privatize the gospel and ignore the fact that social and economic causes, rather than personal sloth or sin, are at the root of world hunger and the nuclear arms race.

Despite the differences between the right and the left in the churches, there have been many examples of prayer as the most potent instrument of action in our own century. The nonviolent civil rights movement under Martin Luther King Jr.'s spiritual leadership was launched and grounded in prayer. The good news remains that prayer does work. And it is no coincidence that the greatest demonstration of unity between black and white came in the prayer-supported civil rights movement.

We now have the glorious precedent that prayer does manifest not only in the kingdom of God with*in* each of us but in the kingdom of God with*out*, in the new society. Dr. King, a model sidewalk contemplative, showed us that prayer not only unites, it purifies and is the only guarantor of a nonviolent victory. Like Gandhi, the chief violence in Dr. King's campaign came from those who assassinated him. Filled with the Spirit, Dr. King's charisma went beyond words. In his very last speech, he showed a freedom from self, and from fear of death, which the Lord had wrought in him.

When I first practiced prayer I prayed only to God, the law of mind action, a totally impersonal God, a life force. I did not even call him Father. These prayers of petition were mostly me, and very little God. When Jesus came to me and revealed that he is God as well as man, there was less of me and more of him in my meditations. I then knew that there were two persons, God the Father and God the Son. One day as I kneeled in urgent prayer, God the Holy Spirit came to me without warning, and in a way that was least expected. To one who had never written a verse, he made himself known in a completely formed verse, a little prayer. I treasure this prayer because it was my first conscious meeting with the Third Person of the Blessed Trinity, the Holy Spirit, and one of my first experiences of the fruits of contemplation. It has been printed and used around the world.

> *Lord, empty me of me,*
> *That I may fill up with Thee.*
>
> *Every minute I've spent on me,*
> *Lord, I now dedicate to Thee.*
>
> *The more the world takes from me,*
> *The more I will produce for Thee.*
>
> *The more perfectly my confidence in Thee,*
> *The more special Thy providence to me.*
>
> *And whatever may happen to me,*
> *I say, Blessed be the Name of Thee.*[10]

Tools for Prayer and Practice to Bring in the Kingdom of God on Earth

1. Put your worship and praise of God first.
2. *Pray* daily: "Thy kingdom come. Thy will be done on earth, as it is in heaven."

3. Say daily Pope John's prayer for the success of Vatican II, Christmas, 1961, quoted above on p. 11.
4. Pray that others will join you in regular fellowship; that the two prayers offered here will build the kingdom, the new society in the world, as well as the new self in the new society.

> Let your kingdom come on earth
> And let it begin in me.

5. Unite in prayer vigils on public and social issues when the Spirit leads you.
6. Heal others in order to heal yourself. Your prayers for the world will give you the last and greatest freedom—freedom from self.
7. Meditate on Jesus Christ's words, quoting the Father: " 'My house shall be called a house of prayer for all nations.' But you have made it a den of robbers" (Mark 11:17).

FOUR

BREAKTHROUGH STEP THREE:
CLEANSING

Step Three: We tried to cleanse ourselves and our society of our defects through prayer and purification, and to make amends for our wrongs—personally and socially (see Acts 5:1–11; Ezek. 16:49–50; Matt. 6:24).

After centuries of privatizing the prophets and the gospel so that only personal sin was stressed, we have belatedly begun to condemn social sin as well. Collective or social sin is now acknowledged by many churches and green-shoots groups. They condemn the war-society and its profiteering, racism, apartheid, and even the maximization of profits with its effect on the poor.

Just as prayer is attending to God, says Evelyn Underhill, the other aspect of the spiritual life, mortification, is dealing with ourselves.[1] And I call mortification and detachment, cleansing. As a guide to cleansing our social sins I have borrowed the seven cleansing steps of Alcoholics Anonymous and revised them for cleansing our *social* rather than just our personal defects (see the last page of this chapter). Of course we have to admit our wrongs, our *social* sins, before we can do anything about them.

The religious in monasteries and convents have always led the world in a collective penance for all our sins. Most of us do not even begin to admit the exact nature of our sins until we are forced to do so. And social sins are even harder to recognize and admit. Has anyone ever taught or exhorted you to confess your social sins? Certainly not school teachers or the average minister or priest. Instead, members of the clergy and teachers alike harangue us for being tardy for school or Mass, for breaking a Lenten fast, or for some other personal infraction. Our great social sins—arrogance to, or exploitation of, those poorer or weaker than ourselves—go unremarked upon. And penance? Most of us relegate this word to the monks and nuns in their cloisters. We seldom even think of penance.

Before I became a Christian I never thought of my captivity in the cold war as an involuntary penance, a personal "refiner's fire" that might purify me. Nor did I see my captivity as a social penance for "the slaughter of innocents" and/or their oppression in the concentration camps and wars of our century, and today's continuing extermination war against the poor. It was only after I became a Christian that I got a glimmer of understanding that, just perhaps, my harassment and hounding by our national security state might become my small penance for what millions suffered *in extremis*.

Just as my pre-Christian penance was involuntary, so was my pre-Christian poverty. As my autobiography tells, I grew up in genteel poverty—bands on my teeth and dancing class but macaroni and cheese on the table. My own work and marriages, however, had brought me several periods of respite from involuntary poverty. One such period was back in the days when I lived as "missus" of our beautiful cattle and all-spice plantation, Rose Hill, on the island of Jamaica. I even had my first and only taste of what it is like to be a member of the landowning ruling class of a white-dominated island.

Though we were poor in cash, we were fairly rich in land and workers—cattlemen, masons, carpenters, all-spice pickers, coconut and lime pickers, and our four house servants. It was a whole new way of life for me. As a child my family could seldom afford a cleaning woman. Mother did the housework with a little help from us as we grew older. But at Rose Hill my husband Jack and I employed more than 100 black men and women in the course of a single year. They depended upon us for their daily breadfruit or yam, their ability to feed their children, their medical care, their clothing, housing, and even the water they drank and bathed in.

As I sat at my typewriter, or prayed, or rode horseback on the green acres of our forested hillside farm, I used to feel vaguely uncomfortable. It was not just the physical discomfort during the first eighteen months of existing without electricity, running hot water, privacy, refrigeration, or driveways. Rather, it was that these Jamaicans got less than a living wage from us. (I knew, because I contributed to the payroll out of my own small salary as north coast correspondent for *The Gleaner*, the island daily.) Their top pay was $8.40 for a six-day workweek, ten hours a day! I felt even more guilty when our black doctor told me that the child of one of our coconut pickers was dying of malnutrition (though he claimed it was a digestive blockage and not hunger). I felt uneasy that my beloved cook, Lillian Buckle, the best private cook on the island, received from us the tiny wage of $6.60 a week. Out of this she had to buy her own food, clothing, and help support her granddaughter.

Back in those days I had two choices as to how to lessen my mental discomfort. I tried to make an issue of it with my Jamaica-born husband. He said that such talk would ruin our precarious hold on the land. The only other alternative was to put on blinders to the poverty of our workers. I could ignore the sight of fifty seasonal allspice pickers hired by the week, sleeping out of doors for lack of shelter, and getting drenched in the rain—all for the few shillings we paid them to pick our crop.

The blinders I put on taught me a great lesson. The only way I could exist in such close proximity with the very poor was by not really seeing their condition. I did not argue when my husband said, "They are not like you and me. They don't mind getting soaked in the rain, or living on yam. That's their way. You can't change them." The lesson I learned was that this is how the owning class of the world constantly blinds and excuses itself: First, don't look at the poverty. Second, if you have to look at it, excuse it on the grounds that the victims are not quite human.

For six years I uneasily went along with these precepts, denying what I saw to prevent the realization that I was living in close quarters with men and women who were undernourished and ragged (some of them walked ten miles each day to and from our farm to work). Nor did I have the excuse of the scions of the inherited rich. They have never known anything other than extracting work from the poor to make them richer. I knew better. I had grown up poor. My father had grown up poor, and my paternal grandfather had grown up poor after the Jacksonian panic of 1837 wiped out the modest prosperity of my great-grandfather. Yet within a few months as a plantation missus I had adjusted not only to the luxury of having four house servants wait upon us but to the blinders of the ruling class. I am glad this happened, for now I can understand how easy it is to fall into the arrogant belief that somehow I am justified in profiting at the expense of my brother and sister.

When I say "forgive me my trespasses," I try to excuse myself for denying the poverty around me during those years on the grounds that I had not met Jesus. Now that I believe in Jesus and his spiritualizing and socializing gospel of "do unto others as you would have them do unto you," I can never again blind myself to exploiting my neighbor.

But how do we account for the blinders worn by Christians in Latin America, in Africa, Europe, and here at home in America? In the neighborhood I live in there are affluent friends who call themselves Christians. Yet many of them remain insensitive to the feelings and conditions of the blacks, migrants, and poor whites who live only a few miles away. Perhaps they do not see them as people. And of course they don't have to see them at all, except for the cleaning woman or the yard man.

We in America sweep our poverty behind the billboards where we don't have to see it. We hide poverty so well with our fast expressways that we are not even aware that it exists. What we don't see does not worry us. Yet when typhoid fever broke out in a Florida migrant camp a few miles away from some of the plushest estates in South Miami, some affluent parents began to experience the golden rule as a practical necessity and not just as a religious precept. A very few even began to take a closer look at the subhuman conditions in which their brothers and sisters around them subsist.

Last winter a friend, Sally Coston, and I did take a closer look. In one day we descended from the heights of opulence at Fort Myers Beach to the pits of poverty at Immokalee, an hour's drive away—going from a winter resort at the season's peak to the outhouses, company stores, shanties, and rags of this migrant and refugee village.

I had visited Florida's Latin migrant camps closer to the gold coast, but now I would be spending a night and a day a mere stone's throw away from the migrants. Our hostess, Sister Maureen Kelleher, R.S.H.M., one of several nuns who serve the Immokalee migrants, is also a lawyer who tries to resolve their knotty legal, employment, housing, and immigration problems.

It was like entering the Third World again. I was back in the Jamaica of the 1950s, seeing in macrocosm what I had lived close to in the microcosm of our farm. From the first stop for directions at the company store (one of two owned by the same men) we were surrounded by smiling, dark-skinned Mexicans, Haitians, Guatemalans, and other migrant groups. After dinner Sister Maureen introduced us to her guests, a Haitian family who hope to go back to Haiti now that Duvalier is out. The next morning we went to Mass at Our Lady of Guadeloupe, a tiny church jammed with white-clad women, a few teenagers in jeans, and many babies. I was happy to see a woman distributing communion, and loved the marvelous music of the guitars and the glorious singing in Spanish. I realized I was seeing the best of Immokalee in this hour of the Sunday Mass.

Sister Maureen, who was the first Green Shoots Award winner of Socially Concerned Contemplatives in 1984, drove us, at my request, around the dusty, sunbaked town. It was like the ghetto in Kingston, Jamaica, only it was a rural ghetto, with tumbledown shacks with outdoor privies, and shanties in which whole families live in one room. There were plenty of bars to drain away the weekly wage, and, of course, processing plants. Most sinister in the blinding sun was the "shape-up" lot, which resembled an execution ground. This is where the crew boss selects the lucky ones who will pile into a rickety old schoolbus and be driven to the fields they will pick.

We saw a nice corner lot with a large one-story house. The crew boss and his family live in it. We saw Sister Maureen's tiny Rural Legal Services office. Reagan was continuing his long attempt to abolish this sole protector the migrants have in the numerous assaults made on them by predatory crew leaders, store owners, and by immigration and naturalization agents.

I recalled my first husband's seminal book on migrants, *America's Own Refugees*,[2] from whose sources I had drawn my own free-lance article in *The Christian Science Monitor*. But Immokalee was the worst rural poverty I had seen since the years in Jamaica. Here in Florida stood the Third World only a few miles in geographical distance but hundreds of miles in conditions from the well-kept mansions of Fort Myers Beach, or the comfortable resorts and middle-class homes on East-West Highway 80.

This shameful poverty was indeed hidden not only behind the billboards, but away from the much-traveled tourist track. In fact, when we drove through the main street of Belle Glade coming and going from Immokalee, we traveled on a beautiful broad street lined with well-nourished royal palm trees. But no longer can the financial and political fathers of Palm Beach county sweep poverty behind the palm trees or the billboards. National publicity spotlights daily the fact that Belle Glade, home of many destitute black workers, has the highest rate of AIDS in the United States, double that of the large cities. A recent test at Belle Glade's health clinic revealed that of 275 clients there, twenty-two volunteers, or 8 percent, had the AIDS antibody in their blood. All were black, twelve were male and ten were female.[3]

Medical researchers outside Palm Beach county have reached the conclusion that it is the incredible wretchedness and filthy living conditions of the poor in Belle Glade that have created a breeding ground for AIDS, because none of the victims can be categorized as either homosexual, hemophiliac, or a drug user. Poverty has existed for years in Belle Glade. More than twenty years ago it was the subject of Edward R. Murrow's famous CBS White Paper, *Harvest of Shame*, which detailed the conditions of farm workers. The documentary was ignored by both growers and politicians in Belle Glade.

Gold coast condominium owners, however, could not ignore the black corpses of fleeing Haitians washed up on their immaculate white-sand beaches. Nor can we as a nation forever sweep our unemployed citizens behind the billboards even as we listen to the bland nightly news that plays down their plight with quotes from the administration minimizing the steady high rate of the jobless. Neither, can we sweep out of sight the poorest of the poor—women, children, the elderly.

Not as frightening, perhaps, as proximity to AIDS, but at the least undesirable has been the involuntary penance exacted from anti-desegregation forces. This penance was commanded by the Supreme Court decision of 1954 ordering the integration of our public schools nearly 100 years after the Civil War was fought to end discrimination. School integration has ripped down the billboards that have hidden the black ghettoes from us whites for the past 100 years. Busing has elicited howls of protest from white parents. But it is an example of the old law that if we don't take the initiative in cleansing and making amends, some type of penance will be forced upon us. This law of justice finds expression both in our personal and collective life. We did not take the initiative in integrating black communities, housing, jobs, and education. The result was a forced penance.

In my personal life I did little to improve the conditions of the poor blacks who worked on our Jamaican farm. Perhaps it was a kind of justice that plunged me into the worst poverty I had ever experienced after leaving the island. Perhaps my personal destitution—lack of medical and dental care and of any income whatever—was a penance, a working out of the cleansing and amends I should have undertaken voluntarily for others as well as myself. When I was denied the right to work by Immigration's deportation order I was not only forced into the greatest penury I had ever known but into utter and total mental insecurity. From 1960 until 1969 I did not know where I would lay my head the next day—whether in North America, Jamiaca, or England.

As a nation all of us have failed to make restitution for the centuries of exploiting blacks. We have reaped what we have sowed in riots, racial hatred, and assassinations. Busing is the very least penance we can offer. And it gets us behind the billboards that hide the poverty of blacks as well as other ethnic groups.

It was Charlotte Spruill who gave me the phrase "we hide our poverty behind the billboards." She did more than that. She and her husband Canon Arthur Spruill of Jacksonville, Florida, formerly lived with their three sons in Delray Beach, where he was assistant rector at St. Paul's Episcopal Church. Charlotte, a professional flutist and composer, volunteered four sessions each week to tutor a young Cuban refugee.

Carlos had been sitting in class for three years without understanding any of his lessons. No one in the public school had taken the time to teach him English. His family was too poor to hire a tutor and too busy with the other ten children to take him to the night classes in English provided for adults. Charlotte, who learned Spanish in her native Texas, went to Carlos's school as soon as her own children went off to their schools. She gave her instruction (and her love) in conversation with Carlos. The formerly failing student not only learned to read but he responded to the love he received by developing his artistic skills as well.

"I am learning much more than Carlos," said Charlotte of her experience. "I get behind the billboard when I visit his family. I see the poverty in which he lives. I gladly accept the busing of my own children as a sort of voluntary atonement for what we all have permitted through our neglect."

There was contagion in Charlotte's person-to-person work. Louise Meade, another Delray wife and mother, soon followed her example by tutoring a black boy at Carlos's school. The work was laid out by the teacher, and Louise did the tutoring in love, as Charlotte had. Louise also gave up her early-morning hours in the summer to drive Carlos to a special summer program when Charlotte was away with her family. These two women were doing more than performing charitable acts; both said they felt they were making some kind of atonement. Charlotte said that children are the innocent victims of the political and economic dislocations that assail their parents.

Of course, if we had not sinned against love in the first place there would be no need for purification. A loving God does not want us constantly beating our breasts in penitential sackcloth and ashes. A loving God has told us he came that we might "have life, and have it more abundantly" (John 10:10). But he wants that abundant life for *each* and *all*, a life abundant in physical goods as well as spiritual riches. This is the kingdom of God on earth. But instead we have lived in and fostered the kingdom of greed. And greed is practiced from the poorest profit-seeking news vendor to the richest millionaire missile manufacturer.

The difference is in the scale of greed, the amount the greedy one gets away with at his level of income. It is a difference in quantity, not quality, since most of us, in Western nations especially, are bred from the cradle upward in the gospel of greed, not the gospel of God. Euphemistically the gospel of greed is called the right to make a profit. The gospel of greed puts profit, property, and power before the individual's spiritual well-being. This upside-down morality is seldom questioned by most of us. We have been born and bred into the belief that we are unpatriotic and un-Christian unless we hold sacred the right to profit and the right to private property. The greedy-grabber gospel envelops all of us from bottom to top. But the poor and the powerless are shut off from profit, property, and power by the dominant elite who give their time, skill, knowledge, care and attention to grabbing and maintaining their fortunes, while flaunting the gains in what Thorstein Veblen called "conspicuous consumption."

The dwindling middle class and multiplying poor cannot compete with the rich in their consumption of yachts, 3,000 pairs of shoes, racehorses, but we can and do swallow whole the gospel of greed. The goal of grabbing material goods as the highest goal is reinforced from our preschool years. Only the exceptional person is nonacquisitive and doesn't want to overdose on food, clothing, houses, and cars. However, I must in all honesty interject the old cliché, "Some of my best friends are rich."

All of us must first admit that we have the greedy-grabber within us. Our unredeemed animal nature is one reason. But add to that the fact that there are profits to be made by catering to the grabber in all of us. Our entire consumer society would fall to pieces in a month if we were all immersed in a behavior modification blitz to "reduce your wants to meet your needs" instead of the present "buy more to live more" attitude we perpetuate.

Even Jesus was not immune to temptations to greed. In the Synoptic Gospels the evil one tempts Jesus with the three most common forms of greed: greed for food, that is greed for material goods; greed for power; and greed for glory (Matt. 4:1–11; Mark 1:13; and Luke 4:1–11). Jesus the man was able to withstand the temptations to greed after John had baptized him with water, and the Father had baptized him in the Spirit. This was also true of the Apostles. They were able to withstand their greedy self-concern, their fears for their own life, status, and safety only after the descent of the Spirit at Pentecost (Acts 2). Saul, the brilliant politician-scholar, became healed of his active greed for fame and power after Jesus converted and blinded him on the road to Damascus (Acts 9). After Paul fasted for three days, Ananias laid hands on him, healing his blindness and baptizing him in the Holy Spirit. Paul followed up his reception of the Spirit, as Jesus had done, by penance and fasting in the desert. Paul also lived, we are told, in voluntary poverty, chastity, and obedience for the rest of his turbulent, redemptive life.

Every one of the world's great religions teaches simple living—the opposite of greed—as a goal. Nuns, brothers, and priests have generally sought to mortify their desire for sex, food, property, power, and money, and not merely as an ascetical discipline but because it is difficult if not impossible to attain union with God through prayer unless one does away with the old self, the greedy-grabber.

Voluntary poverty, however, does not imply destitution. Rather, it is the decision not to be possessed by the desire for money or goods. And today many religious practitioners live in comfortable houses or apartments and wear decent clothes. Their housing is so removed from the impoverished that on visiting my simple apartment in Florida, one nun commented: "You are the one who really lives simply, almost in poverty. How wonderful! " I couldn't share her enthusiasm because I wish I could afford more space for work, dining, and storage (and my cat), and more mechanization, such as a word processor or even a washing machine.

A bridge between personal asceticism and that offered for social justice is the fasting practice of the *Cursillo* movement. This "little course in Christianity" (the translation of *Cursillo*) was brought to Mexican migrants in Texas by Spanish pilots in the early 1960s. The Mexicans followed the crops north to Michigan, where I became one of the first Anglo women in the Midwest to make a *Cursillo* in 1963. The male *cursillistas*, largely priests, offered to make *palanca*— in other words, fast and pray for the success of my *Cursillo*. A palanca is a lever. And their lever did give me inspiration and perseverance. It was an arduous but fruitful experience for me and the thousands who followed us.

Fasting as a means of bringing about social justice had, of course, been practiced before Gandhi. But the most successful fast for social change in the twentieth-century was led by the scrawny, dark-skinned Hindu. Steeped in the gospel of Jesus, Gandhi followed his example in purifying and cleansing himself from all forms of greed. Day after day his followers suffered vicariously, and some in practice, as Gandhi all but starved himself to death in British prisons or at his own monastic-like abode. Day after day prayers went up throughout India for his release. Those prayers, combined with Gandhi's cleansing fasts and prayer meetings, did more to bring about the liberation of India than any purely political act committed by secular independence leaders. Gandhi also fasted to abolish the caste system in India and some of the horrifying superstitions within the ranks of his own people, such as the cruelties toward the "untouchables."

Nearly three decades before Gandhi fasted for social change, British suffragists led by Emmeline Pankhurst initiated a hunger strike when they were jailed for militant action in their struggle to win from Parliament the right to vote. The story of their magnificent courage is told in the book and documentary film *Shoulder to Shoulder*, which is graphic in its portrayal of the forced feeding tubes being pushed down their protesting throats. Though they would not win the vote for many more years (not until 1928, in fact), they did make two American converts who shared their British jail cells.

Back home in the United States these American feminists, Alice Paul and Lucy Burns, demonstrated that they had learned well the militant tactics of their British sisters. Along with their followers, they threw the first picket line in history around the White House in 1917, demanding the vote. They camped across from the White House in Lafayette Park. They were arrested in droves, 268 of them, and sent to one of the worst jails in the country, Occoquan workhouse. There Alice and Lucy led their Main Line cohorts as well as factory workers and a young journalist, Dorothy Day, in a hunger strike. Prison officials force-fed them, repeating the sufferings of their British sisters. Nationwide headlines gave more publicity to the suffrage cause in jail than did any of the parades, meetings, conventions, or testimonies on Capitol Hill. And they won! Congress approved the Nineteenth Amendment to the Constitution (popularly known as the Susan B. Anthony Amendment) and sent it to the thirty-six states, which had ratified it by August 26, 1920.

Since then the political hunger strike has been used in many movements to bring about radical social change. Among its champions have been such civil rights leaders as Ralph Abernathy and Dick Gregory. Mitch Snyder of the Community for Creative Nonviolence, the United States champion of the homeless, fasted nigh unto death to keep his homeless charges from being thrown from their shabby shelter a stone's throw from the White House out into the cold streets. Boycotts (a fast from buying *and* eating) have been used by Cesar Chavez, the Roman Catholic leader of the United Farm Workers Union. Nonunion grapes and lettuce disappeared from the tables of some of the Catholic hierarchy and religious, and the rich and not so rich who joined the boycott.

Religious congregations of women and men have divested themselves of antisocial investments in apartheid South Africa, and, closer to home, in the U.S. slums, ghettos, and war plants. The pioneer in consumer awareness as distinct from political boycotts is Ralph Nader. He exposed the perils of the American automobile when he burst upon the national scene and has consistently directed sober and compelling studies upon which consumers' action could be based if they were sufficiently organized. Ralph himself, it is reported, leads a frugal life, almost monklike, and has been a model of simple living.

In today's church some of the Catholic hierarchy live simply. Bishop Manuel Larrain Errzuriz of Talca, Chile, president of CELAM, gave church lands to house the poor.[4] This was before the overthrow of the assassinated Allende's government by a military coup. Chilean bishops, along with CELAM, acted in conformity with their brother bishops from around the globe, who published their Synod's consensus in the forthright and progressive *Justice in the World*. I often wonder how many Catholics have ever read this call for a transformation of the world.[5]

In it they wrote:

> . . . we . . . perceive the serious injustices which are building around the world of men a network of domination, oppression and abuses which stifle freedom and which keep the greater part of humanity from sharing in the building up and enjoyment of a more just and more fraternal world."

But the bishops also see

> the inmost stirring moving the world in its depths. . . . In associations of men and among people themselves there is arising a new awareness which shakes them out of any fatalistic resignation and which spurs them on to liberate themselves and to be responsible for their own destiny.[6]

The document calls for education to justice and deplores the "narrow individualism" that is still encouraged:

> Part of the human family lives immersed in a mentality which
> exalts possessions. . . . But education demands a renewal of
> heart, a renewal based on the recognition of sin in its individ-
> ual and social manifestations. It will likewise awaken a critical
> sense, which will lead us to reflect on the society in which we
> live and on its values; it will make men ready to renounce
> these values when they cease to promote justice for all men.[7]

The bishops point to First World countries, saying: "In societies enjoying a higher level of consumer spending, it must be asked whether
our life-style exemplifies that sparingness with regard to consumption which we preach to others as necessary in order that so many
millions of hungry people throughout the world may be fed."[8]

Yet some, like retired Bishop Helder Camaro of Olinda-Recif,
Brazil, and many younger priests in the Americas—South and Central—actually share the poverty of their parishioners in the rural
areas as well as the barrios. They are living up to the Synod's statement: ". . . our faith demands a certain sparingness in use, and the
Church is obliged to live and administer its own goods in such a
way that the Gospel is proclaimed to the poor. If instead the Church
appears to be among the rich and the powerful of this world its
credibility is diminished."[9]

Protestant churches have long carried the message of social justice
through their own clergy. Frederick Herzog, United Church of
Christ pastor and a faculty member of the Duke University Divinity
School, says in his book *Justice Church*: ". . . a pastor who is not involved in God's battle against poverty has no authority in the pulpit
or otherwise. A Christian not participating in God's battle has no
power to bring others to Christ . . . poverty is the touchstone of so
much else; poverty breeds crime. It is the foil of greed and hardness
of heart."[10]

The author in 1970 of the first North American book on liberation
theology, Dr. Herzog states ten years later that the Bible "very effectively pointed out that God does not consider poverty a natural phenomenon. Poverty was not something to be stoically endured. . . ."[11]

He continues, "... those who read the Bible ought to have been able to see that the poor and oppressed have a claim on justice.... Liberation theology deals with God's persistent struggle for justice and the tenacious human struggle against oppression in the last quarter of the twentieth century."[12]

Part of that struggle consists of what Brazilian educator Paulo Freire calls "cultural actions" as distinct from more speeches, more seminars, more lobbying on Capitol Hill. Freire says that a cultural action seeks to "clarify to the oppressed the objective situation which binds them to oppressors, visible or not."[13] I am not suggesting we give up meetings, speeches, or lobbying. What I am asking is that we at least consider the boycott as a means to a very specific end.

If even for one day large coalitions of people boycotted every store, shop, shopping mall, restaurant, market, and gas station, their demands would be met sooner or later. No one has tried this. But Father Thomas J. Reese, associate editor of *America* magazine, said in 1983 from another point of view: "What I have in mind is shutting down the world for 24 hours. People would stay in their homes... using no utilities ... and spend the time in prayer and reading the Scriptures as a family.... Such a labor-hunger strike would be a spiritual cry to God and a political cry to world leaders to do something about peace."[14]

One result of the One Day Buyers' Boycott I am suggesting would be the education of those of us who organize it and participate fully in it to reduce our own wants to meet our needs. Religious and secular activists alike would require a minimum of six months lead time to win adherents and mobilize the action. Uniting with hundreds of groups, we could set up prayer and picket lines outside all retail establishments (including the banks), not to penalize them but simply to let them know the power of our purse. Our platform *against* poverty and *for* peace would be broad enough for the coalition.

One day spent on such a boycott, praying and picketing, would educate not only the retail establishments but the public. However, even a nonviolent prayer-picket line of women, men, and children would probably draw the hostility common to such actions, and perhaps even the kind of violence reported on television news. I learned both these facts while marching with 2,000 women to the gates of the Seneca Falls army depot, protesting the deployment of Pershing and Cruise missiles in 1983. We in the religious task force were chosen to march ahead with our prayers and hymns. We were Christians with the Bible, Sufis, United Church of Christ leaders, and members of other denominations. We had been holding prayer vigils outside the gates of the depot. Now we were in the front line for the expected violence as we marched and stood for nine hours. We had the help of Governor Cuomo through former congress-woman Bella Abzug, one of our participants, in getting the pro-tection of the National Guard in stopping threatened attacks from our opponents. We therefore had no eggs and stones thrown at us, nor shots fired. But we did have questions thrown at us, and pic-tures shot by a score of press persons.

Our brothers and sisters were not so lucky on March 22, 1986 in a tiny rally (200) in Miami against Reagan's $100,000,000 demands to arm further the *contra* war he is waging against the Nicaraguan government. A near riot of 2,000 pro-*contras* took place because Miami Mayor Xavier Suarez had given a militant pro-*contra*, anti-Castro organization a permit to demonstrate at the same place at the same time. The mayor himself never "strayed from the pro-*contra* side of the block,"[15] wrote the Miami *Herald*. In fact, he gave a five-minute speech condemning as "Marxist groups" the state legis-lators, Quakers, a city commissioner, and the other peace demon-strators. The riot had been stimulated, the *Herald* said, by anti-Castro radio stations whipping up a frenzy as soon as they learned of the permit granted the peaceful, anti-*contra* group. Pro-*contra* Cubans carrying eggs and rocks hurled a rock that hit one of the Crisis team officials. The 200 peace demonstrators could only retreat to their own cars, because they were escorted by police who bused them.[16]

I give this example of violence in Miami, because a national One Day Buyers' Boycott prayer-picket line might be met with the same or worse opposition. Antijustice and antipeace forces can be whipped to the same frenzy of hate by electronic ministers and the drummers for the corporate state.

The same kind of careful preparation that was given at the Seneca Falls Women's Peace Encampment must be given to all prayer picketers. *Non*violent response to violence is an acquired action. Hymns and prayer are hard to maintain when eggs are sopping your face and dress, or a rock hurtles toward your head. Even the Miami riot squad, according to the *Herald*, was not able to quell the violence the 2,000 rioters directed against the 200 peace demonstrators.[17]

Our One Day Buyers' Boycott might also give some of us an inkling of what William James in *The Varieties of Religious Experience* called "the moral equivalent of war." James said that war is the only action calling forth the ascetical drive that is in all of us. Of course in 1902 he was writing of prenuclear war, the foot soldier, the cavalry officer. Today all of us are victims of war.

Of the earlier warfare James said: "What we now need to discover in the social realm is the moral equivalent of war; something heroic that will speak to men as universally as war does, and yet will be compatible with their spiritual selves as war has proved itself to be incompatible."[18]

It is no coincidence that AA's Bill Wilson had steeped himself in these pages. Of all the twentieth-century fellowships, institutions, organizations, societies, and churches in existence, AA is the only one I know that conforms to James's idea of a "moral equivalent of war." For the alcoholic to give up booze, which to him or her is dearer than life, is an act one could call heroic. AA is certainly though not religious for its members "compatible with their spiritual selves...."[19] Finally, AA is the "strenuous life" ... without the brass bands or uniforms or hysterical popular applause or lies of circumlocutions ..." of war.[20]

Before the founding of AA, Moral Rearmament, or the Oxford Movement, as it was also called, had already tried to become a moral equivalent of war. But I think it lacked the humbling, bracing tradition of anonymity. Not only are there no brass bands in AA, there are no big names, no big shot leaders. AA itself can neither own property nor lend its name to anything. It is a poor society that cannot accept big grants or contributions. It exists on the quarters and dollars put in the basket at meetings. For more than fifty years it has flourished in its single task of helping alcoholics to recover. At any given time, AA has more than a million sober members.

I would even describe AA as actually counterculture. While the rest of the Western world is bent on consumerism or maximization of profits, AA demands a voluntarily accepted corporate poverty along with its anonymity. James said that when he sees the way "wealth getting enters as an ideal into the very bone and marrow of our generation, one wonders whether a revival of the belief that poverty is a worthy religious vocation may not be 'the transformation of military courage' and the spiritual reform which our time stands most in need of."[21]

Neither James nor this book is advocating the *in*voluntary poverty rampant today. There is no virtue in hunger and homelessness that are forced upon one. But—and this remains as true today as it was eighty-five years ago—only voluntary poverty, a true indifference to wealth, enables one to champion an unpopular cause. A person for whom poverty has no terrors is a free person, James said. Again, I would add that it would have to be a poverty voluntarily accepted.

With the exception of Alcoholics Anonymous and other societies that seek simpler living, we in 1986 are much farther away from James's vision of the moral equivalent of war than the world was in 1902. Our leaders tell us that we can have both bombs and butter, bribing us, they think, into acceptance of the arms race. But can we have both?

Indeed, can even a socialist state, the Soviet Union, have both bombs and butter? My experience of two trips there in 1982 and 1984 suggest that the answer is no. In fact, on my last evening in Moscow in 1984, the impact of the nuclear arms race was evident in the poorly dressed Muscovites scurrying under their cheap umbrellas to stand in long lines to buy skimpy vegetables, fruit, and meat.

The Soviets are poor in consumer goods both because of the arms race and the West's head start of nearly 200 years of industrialization. But I learned that as poor as they are in consumer goods, they do have free medical care as well as freedom from unemployment and hunger. The United States, with all its great industrial capacity that could, if utilized, feed, house, and clothe the world, is poorer than the other major industrialized nations—socialist or capitalist—in social services.

It is time for us to enhance our awareness of these defects in our society instead of lying about them or hiding them. A One Day Buyers' Boycott could start *conscientization* among the middle class— an awareness of the greedy-grabber within all of us, and a determination that we must not privatize our services to the poor, as conservatives are recommending. Instead, we must multiply our public services.

Dr. Herzog wrote: "If God considered poverty the right and natural way for the majority to live in the world, he would not have inspired Mary to sing in the Magnificat, 'He has put down the mighty from their thrones, and exalted those of low degree; he has filled the hungry with good things, and the rich he has sent empty away'"[22] (Luke 1:52–53).

Tools to Abolish the Greedy-Grabber in Ourselves and Our Society

1. Practice step three of Breakthrough.
   We tried to cleanse ourselves and our society of our defects through prayer and purification, and to make amends for our wrongs—personally and socially.
2. Start today to take the seven cleansing steps of Alcoholics Anonymous as I have revised them for the cleansing of *social* rather than personal defects alone:

   AA step four. We made a searching and fearless moral inventory of ourselves as nation and world.

   AA step five. Admitted to God, to ourselves, and to another human being the exact nature of our social sins.

   AA step six. Were entirely ready to have God remove all these defects in our society.

AA step seven. Humbly asked him to remove our society's short-comings.
AA step eight. Made a list of persons, groups, classes, races, nations we had harmed and became willing to make amends to them all.
AA step nine. Made direct amends to such people and groups whenever possible, except when to do so would injure them.
AA step ten. Continued to take personal and social inventory, and when we were wrong, promptly admitted it.

More tools for cleansing and amends:

3. Start today to curb your own greediness for food, power, money, clothes, houses, gadgets, cars, booze, pills, cigarettes. Greed has been inculcated in us from childhood wherever we are on the economic ladder. Practice its opposite—detachment from "things" and poverty of the spirit.
4. Fast from goods and services produced in conditions contrary to gospel morality (Sermon on the Mount, Matt. 5–7). Do the best you can on this tool. [Only those living in special self-contained communes could practice step three all the way without starving or going naked.]
5. Reduce your wants to meet your needs.
6. "Forgive us our trespasses as we forgive those who trespass against us."
7. Read and meditate upon the following New Testament texts on the right use of material goods: Luke 3:11, Luke 10:30–37; Mark 12:41–44; James 5:1–6; I Tim. 6:8–10; Eph. 4:28; 2 Cor. 8:13–15; I John 3:17; Acts 2:44–45 and Acts 4: 32–36.

FIVE.

BREAKTHROUGH STEP FOUR:
VISION

Step Four: We obtained a vision of the best the world could be—
the kingdom of God, the new society that God plans for us.

The classic name for this stage in the individual's personal breakthrough is "illumination." It generally arrives after the start of the
three stages of spiritual growth described in the chapters on admission and awakening, prayer, and cleansing. I entered the illuminative
stage with my conversion to Jesus Christ as Lord. For me this was the
beginning of five years of floating in the spaceship of oneness with
him described in Chapter 1. During those years my life was also illu-
minated by accepting friends, loving teachers, and my spiritual guide,
Father Louis Putz.

I believe that the illuminative stage began in the *world* when Jesus
launched the kingdom of God on earth, and for two centuries following his resurrection the young Christian church was marked by
love and holiness. In fact, elements of the early Christian community
became the model for most future helping institutions, organizations,
and even nations.

Friedrich Engels, the coauthor with Karl Marx of *The Communist
Manifesto*, and his lifelong coworker, quoted the French Communists as saying: "If I wanted to give you an idea of the early Christian
communities I would tell you to look at a local section of the International Working Men's Association" (the forerunner of the Com-

munist International).[1] And in the twentieth century, Nikita Khrushchev reportedly said, "There could be no communism without Christianity preceding it."[2] Khrushchev's words have been interpreted to mean that the persecuted, underground life of the young church hiding in the catacombs was the model for future revolutionary groups.

One of my earliest visions of the kingdom of God in our society came to me several years before I met Jesus. I called this vision "the love bomb." It grew out of an interview I had in Key West with a yachtsman. This yachtsman had struck it rich while putting the United States in the forefront of the nuclear arms race. But far from rejoicing in his newlyfound wealth, the nuclear millionaire was living on the edge of perpetual fear. Goaded by his fear of retribution—that the increased slaughter made possible by his discovery would destroy him along with the United States—he bought and outfitted a large yacht for himself, his wife, and their three children. He became a modern-day Noah with his lavishly equipped "ark." He not only stowed on board all kinds of antiradioactive medical supplies, but also high-tech communications with shore designed to check radiation levels in the event of a nuclear disaster. "We can stay at sea for six months," he told me, "without touching shore after any nuclear explosion."

I felt sorry for this man and his family, recalling Jesus' saying, "What does a man gain by winning the whole world at the cost of his true self?" (Mark 8:36, NEB) My vision transformed him (in a play never produced) from a guilt-ridden millionaire to a physicist I called Adam. Adam's job was to make the final check on an H bomb that the United States planned to explode on a troublesome Caribbean island. The island was to serve as a guinea pig for intensive studies and investigations of the effects of blast and radiation on all tropical life.

Adam, though usually meticulous in his work, happened to be dreaming of his new beloved at the time he did his final check of the bomb. Emotions of love and goodwill permeated his every cell, tissue, organ, action, and function. Then he accompanied the expedition of scientists, military personnel, and journalists to a safe vantage point away from the doomed island. He was in the landing party when the island was considered safe following the nuclear blast. The officials had all been briefed on the anticipated scenes of death and devastation. But instead of the stillness of death they heard fifes, drums, and human voices. Instead of carnage they saw black and white men, women and children just above the palm-fringed beach dancing, singing, and holding their arms out to the landing party in a joyous welcome.

The stunned landing party refused the roast breadfruit, curried goat, and rum that was offered until they tested samples from the debris of the mysteriously nonlethal, though exploded, bomb. Finally they accepted the food and drink, and joined in the dancing. One of them thought to send a cable to the commander in chief in Washington about the miracle of the nuclear "dud" and they put together a story (that happened to be correct). The journalistic pool got its cable out to editors around the world, Adam's love had transformed the killer bomb into a "love bomb," said one smart journalist. The tag and the practice became universal, and everyone lived happily ever after in a love-bombed world.

This vision has persisted since it first came to me. I pray the words "love bomb" to transform a person, scene, place, or event. Driving past an ominous looking entrance to an army arsenal, I love-bombed it into a colony for artists and their children, who choose life, not death, and create beauty rather than pain. Or I love bomb grim-faced, bored adults into happy, smiling children who are watching Flipper the porpoise dive into her tank on the Florida Keys. I can at times get myself out of the way enough to love-bomb feared relatives, such as a former mother-in-law. I was able to transform her rather stern face into the wistful teenage wallflower I knew she had been. Then I could feel compassion for her, not fear.

But large-scale vision is needed for the problems that beset not just individuals but society. Both the prophets and the gospel have given us such warnings and hope. "Where there is no vision, the people perish" (Prov. 29:18). The prophets wrote down their visions,

"The wolf shall dwell with the lamb, and the leopard shall lie down with the kid. . . . They shall not hurt or destroy in all my holy mountain. . . ." (Isa. 11:6, 9) Long ago they wrote the text engraved at the United Nations today ". . . and they shall beat their swords into plowshares, and their spears into pruning hooks" (Isa. 2:4; Mic. 4:3).

On the day of Pentecost when the Spirit descended upon the Apostles, they began putting into practice Jesus' vision of the kingdom in the Sermon on the Mount. In the twinkling of an eye the spirit transformed the Apostles from defecting cowards to bold evangelizers empowered to love-bomb the rest of the known world. Describing how the community actually lived, St. Luke wrote: "There was not a needy person among them, for as many as were possessors of lands or houses sold them, and brought the proceeds of what was sold and laid it at the apostles' feet; and distribution was made to each as any had need" (Acts 4:34–35).

The punishment of death was instantaneous for any who, like Ananias and Sapphira, tried to make a profit, holding back for their own use the price they received for their private property instead of giving it to the common good, the church (Acts 5:1–11). These passages in Acts, which are ignored by most preachers, evangelists and even theologians, form a biblical foundation for the distinctive mark of early Christianity: distribution of goods according to need, not according to greed or profit. But resistance to social change is stubborn. The kingdom of greed is still winning the battle against the kingdom of God. Today it manifests on an unprecedented scale in the maximized profits reaped from the nuclear arms race.

In this time of trauma and nuclear panic we need to have not only visions of the kingdom of God to sustain us but perspectives on life. These vistas offer an alternative to blotting it all out with some form of anesthesia. They are history, perspective on the past; hope, perspective on the future; and humor, perspective on the present. Each of us can get in touch with our own personal history. This is one of the great psychological advances of our century. Today it has become almost commonplace for us to reflect upon and share our personal histories in groups for alcoholics, drug addicts, the overweight, neurotics, and gamblers. Therapists encourage their clients to keep journals and write their personal histories at retreats, rehabilitation centers, or in private or clinical practice; dream histories are often recorded. The days of childhood amnesia are gone. And of course in the vanguard of telling personal history are the professional writers who have explored every nook and cranny of their lives, some starting with their prenatal days. Libraries and bookstores are crowded with personal histories from convicts to nuns, from film stars to hired help at the White House.

There is, however, a dearth of writing about the movers and shakers who changed the course of history in the first half of the twentieth century. Even in a well-stocked university library it is hard to find many biographies or accounts of the Populists, "Wobblies," Socialists, or Communists, who were a crucial political force from 1900 until the interruptions of World War I and II and the cold war silenced them. Public television occasionally shows documentaries on the start of the CIO in the thirties, or Great Depression films that have become more pertinent in the 1980's epidemic of poverty. But mention to a class of undergraduates, or even graduates, at universities the names of such historical figures as "Big Bill" Haywood, Norman Thomas, Elizabeth Gurley Flynn, Emma Goldman, "Mother" Bloor, and there is a dead silence. There are exceptions to the blank tablets of the students' minds: the civil rights movement in the 1960s and 1970s (this retrieved some of the unknown or lost black history); and the revival of the women's movement in the 1960s, which began to rescue women and their works from near blackout. It was because of this blackout that my Aunt Susan took on the hated task of sitting down with her colleagues in 1876 to collate and/or write the massive, four Volume *History of Woman Suffrage*. She would far have preferred to be on the road in action for the cause. It took her nearly fifteen years of driving her collaborators to meet deadlines and getting the necessary funds before the first volume could be published.

Recently I had a chance to review some of women's roots when I was asked to give a commencement address on the subject "The Legacy of Risk." I didn't have to look far in my own family. Among the other risks Aunt Susan took in the cause of women's suffrage was her first feminist act of civil disobedience, illegal voting. This took place nearly a century before the arrest and imprisonment of Gandhi, Dorothy Day, and Martin Luther King, Jr. Among male risk takers is Eugene Debs, labor leader and a candidate for the presidency in 1912, who got almost one million votes for the Socialist party. But under the World War I Sedition Act the great hero of the labor movement was arrested because he gave an antiwar speech. He was sentenced to ten years in jail, a death sentence to a body already damaged by years of service to labor. He died shortly after release.

John Reed was rescued from obscurity (except in his own hometown Portland, Oregon) in the epic film *Reds*, 1982. The dashing Harvard-educated foreign correspondent wrote the classic *Ten Days That Shook the World*, which remains the best short history of the Russian Revolution. The film *Reds* is both a visual and an audio history of the radical social change in the first two decades of our century. Reed risked and gave his life for socialism, which he had embraced after being jailed in the violence of the silk workers' strike.

When the Bolsheviks overthrew the moderate Kerensky regime on November 7, 1917, Reed was in the right place at the right time, in Leningrad. His first hand reporting remains a model of historical journalism. He and the other risk takers have given us a social and economic perspective on how our world came to be, at the brink of the broken connection with history. They've even given us badly needed hope.

Fortunately the quality of hope does not rest solely on what we see in this crumbling shell of the old secular society—a shell that is being penetrated by the new society. Pierre Teilhard de Chardin and other Christian evolutionists see hope not as limited to our personal hope but as God's hope. Teilhard says that humanity can march forward only if it has a "great hope in common." One of the century's leading prophets of hope for the living, he influenced succeeding prophets, as we have seen, including Pope John XXIII. Pope John insisted that Jesus proclaimed the gospel to men and women living today—the poor, the homeless, the oppressed. Teilhard taught that despair is the tool of the enemy within ourselves, our country, and our world.

A personal link with Teilhard is my longtime friend, Nobel Peace Prize nominee Helen Foster Snow, whose autobiography, *My China Years*, is being made into a TV miniseries. Nearly fifty years ago she became the first woman to publish her personal interviews with the Chinese Communist leaders Mao and Chou in the classic *Inside Red China*.[3] With her late husband Edgar Snow (*Red Star Over China*),[4] Helen helped build détente between her native United States and the emerging People's Republic of China as far back as 1938. She and Edgar Snow founded, with Rewi Ally, the Chinese Industrial Cooperatives. They are honored as the first authors to publish living history as it was made by the leaders of the Chinese Communists' struggle to establish the People's Republic of China.

Journeying from the opposite ends of the earth, Helen Snow and Teilhard, two of the leading convergent and creative thinkers of our century, met in China to walk and talk atop the Tartar Wall overlooking the rooftops of Peking in the 1930s. They were not unmindful that their talk, their writings, and their deeds might have an impact on the world beyond those rooftops—to the south, the north, the east, and the west.

Until his death the church banned Teilhard not only from teaching in the universities of France but from publishing any of his words (the worst silencing for a writer), including his masterpiece, *The Phenomenon of Man*. Helen Snow, like Teilhard, has the gift I call "cosmic optimism." She believes that the new self and the new society must emerge simultaneously from the shell of the old. Helen influenced Teilhard's thought in that she, the young, glamorous American journalist, served as a rare and responsive sounding board for his new ideas. And she in turn readily admits his influence. He poured out to her his evolutionary theories and his syntheses. Even then, he saw the urgent need for advanced Christian ethics in science because of the danger of technology allowed to run riot in war societies. Teilhard urges us: "The Age of Nations is past. The task before us now, if we would not perish, is to build the earth."[5]

History may be dimmed and hope flicker low, but there is another perspective to help us in this time of trauma. It is humor. I call humor the little sister of joy—the fruit of the Spirit. Even though I could never emulate my joy-filled prayer partners at charismatic meetings, I always admired them. Go to any open meeting of Alcoholics Anonymous and you will find laughter as well as love-in-action, and sharing. Alcoholics and their friends laugh at themselves as they tell their histories. Outsiders say, "How can you bear to laugh at the awful things you did and those that happened to you? I should think you'd cry." AA would answer, "Since we are not going to drink today we can laugh at ourselves, even rejoice in our sobriety. We cried when we knew we were going to get drunk all over again." So they laugh frequently and delightedly at themselves.

Like most of you, I have had moments of joy, sheer joy. But they have not been sustained. And we can't pump up and train ourselves in joy. But we *can* consciously cultivate her little sister, humor, just as some of us have consciously cultivated gratitude, the little sister of humility. I have even collected some aids to humor over the years. I keep a "laugh gallery," a file folder with notes on funny things that have happened to me on my way through life. I pull them out when all about me is war hysteria or depression. And though Reagan is no laughing matter with his frightening rhetoric, I savor any satire or spoof on the White House residents and other politicians.

Can one still laugh at reruns of *Dr. Strangelove or: How I Learned to Stop Worrying and Love the Bomb*? Yes. If we don't laugh we shall either break down or burn out as we work hard to win even the modest goals for peace sought today. We must rejoice that today we are alive and not atomized. Professional humor is a major casualty of the cold war. Try and find today a good political satire—live or on television. Try and find a stand-up socially aware comedian to give a few minutes' surcease from the controlled panic of the times.

Aside from Mark Russell, who is there? That is why we need to nurture our own humor and pray for humor's big sister, joy. Realize that you are following in the footsteps of some of the saints who enjoyed "the high spirits peculiar to high spirituality." Their laughter was a protection against the Evil One, according to Professor R. C. Zaehner, who wrote: ". . . one thing Satan cannot simulate, and that is joy—joy without which all sanctity is void."[6]

In the nuclear age, though we tend to ignore joy as a fruit of the Spirit, we can at least practice humor in order to give perspective on ourselves. It may even lead to freedom *from* self. The great mystical doctor of the church, St. Teresa of Avila, showed her humor not only in her books but as she went about her duties at the convent singing happily. She even composed ditties such as this one:

> *Let nothing disturb thee,*
> *Nothing affright thee;*
> *All things are passing;*
> *God never changeth.*[7]

We need not only perspective and visions of the new society to inspire us but models—models of the kingdom of God "on earth, as it is in heaven," models of the best the world *could* be. The history of any century since Jesus is written in the lives of individuals and communities who radiated the light of love and hope. Among these groups and individuals, the following are most notable:

1. Jesus and the apostolic church before and after his resurrection until Constantine's conversion, 313 A.D.

2. The Communion of Saints: ". . . The Body of Christ . . . in which each Christian has his individual part to play in harmony with the whole, and which, lives by the breath of the Holy Spirit and the blood of Christ, which, through the sacrament of the Eucharist, feeds the individual cells and nourishes the whole. . . ." This is ". . . what we mean by the Communion of Saints, and it is the hidden aspiration of all mankind."[8]

3. After Constantine's conversion, monastic communities began structuring religious life. The Benedictines followed by other religious communities have provided a 1,400-year witness to the world that communities based on production and distribution according to need, not greed, can succeed—especially when combined with love, ethics, and discipline.

4. Religious societies such as the Friends of God in the fourteenth century, the Society of Friends, founded in the seventeenth century (known as the Quakers), the Mennonites, the Shakers, and many other organizations of devout men and women formed structured communities even when they had little or no liturgy. The Quakers, "plain people," have always been in the forefront of peace and the movement for social justice, while the Salvation Army and others have rallied to the poor on a one-to-one basis.

5. Utopian communities portrayed in *Looking Backward* and other works; utopian societies such as Oneida and Lilydale.

6. Prayer-share groups and retreats since the 1950s, especially the Anglican Fellowship of Prayer, founded by Canon and Mrs. Sam Shoemaker in the United States and abroad; the U.S. Catholic-led prayer group movement, later to become the worldwide charismatic movement, founded by some of us at Saint Mary's College, Notre Dame, and Notre Dame University in 1965; the non-Catholic charismatic renewal in mainstream Protestant churches; the contemplative renewal in groups founded in England and Canada by Dom John Main, O.S.B., and in the United States by Abbot Keating, of the Cistercian order.

7. The House of Prayer proliferation, begun in the late sixties and continuing into the eighties, was started by both secular and religious leaders.

8. Residential communities of charismatics—the Church of the Redeemer in Houston, and the "households" at Ann Arbor, Michigan, and South Bend, Indiana; charismatic colleges such as Steubenville, Ohio.

9. Longtime retreat and revival movements of the Protestants and camps, especially in the South. Nationally there are the Camps

Farthest Out and the social justice-oriented compound at Kirkridge in Pennsylvania.

10. "L'Arche" of Jean Vanier for retarded adults.

11. Alcoholics Anonymous, the oldest, largest, and most innovative, model of a nonreligious but spiritual community.

12. "Green shoots under the nuclear mushroom": Since 1974 I have been keeping notes on these signs of hope for social as well as personal change. They are like the green shoots that spring up, reaching for air and light, under the mushrooms in the dark woods that I have walked and ridden in. They give us hope whether we are Catholic, Protestant, or Jewish. But we cannot sustain hope without prayer—prayer while marching, prayer while picketing, prayer in our own rooms, and prayer before the altar. For it is only God who can save us from the burnout that sometimes wipes out champions of peace and justice. In fact, hope built up by prayer is what distinguishes sidewalk contemplatives from secular activists. Rabbi Abraham Heschel described his nonviolent protest in Selma, standing for hours with the others, by saying, "I prayed with my feet."

For the most part, green shoots are postnuclear. The major exception is the mother of them all, the Catholic Worker movement, founded in 1933 by Dorothy Day and Peter Maurin. Green shoots are popping up all over the world today, "first the blade, then the ear, then the full grain in the ear" (Mark 4:28). Green shoots generally advocate "a preferential option for the poor;" nonviolence, and a structured spiritual and intellectual life as well as demonstrations and cultural actions.

13. The Spirit does blow where it will, planting green shoots among evangelicals. The Sojourner community and magazine have provided leadership for social change since the group's inception. Its annual celebration of Peace Pentecost grew to nonviolent civil disobedience with a pray-in at the U.S. Capitol in 1983, leading to arrests.

14. A social justice lobby of sisters in 1971, a truly innovative idea, was launched by Sister Carol Coston, O.P., and forty-five

other sisters. NETWORK seeks to "make Congress more responsive to the needs of all people . . . the poor, the powerless, and the marginalized . . . and to promote world peace, justice and equality." NETWORK is based not on "frenetic short-term political action, but rather on a long-term commitment to change through the legislative, political process." Our first Socially Concerned Contemplatives national Green Shoots Award was made to one of the early leaders of NETWORK, Sister Maureen Kelleher, R.S.H.M., for her work of nearly fifteen years with the lobby.

15. Another green shoot is Center for Concern, focusing on a "world that is human." It organizes conferences on religion and labor, on hunger, and on women in the church.

16. The lively, versatile Quixote Center in nearby Maryland drew national attention when its investigation of the Karen Silkwood death led to a verdict against the nuclear plant, Kerr-McGee, in Oklahoma. The court finally awarded $10,000,000 to the surviving family, setting a national precedent and giving hope to other nuclear-contaminated workers and their families. Upheld by the U.S. Supreme Court, the decision is an important one. The list of the center's involvement ranges from Sister Maureen Fiedler's founding of Catholics Act for ERA in the 1970s to the 1986 Quest for Peace program launched by staffer Father Bill Callaghan, S.J., with Bishop Thomas Gumbleton of Detroit as chair.

17. Mobilizing the fastest growing population group, the elderly of America (especially women), is the Reverend Louis J. Putz, C.S.C., of Notre Dame, who celebrated his golden jubilee as a priest in 1986. Keeping the minds and hearts of elders green are his program Harvest House and its educational arm, Forever Learning. In the latter, retired professors teach retired women and men in classes that range from bridge to theology. He and longtime, executive director Harriet Kroll, along with their volunteer leaders have been so successful that the bishop of Phoenix invited Father Putz to establish a second program there.

The six-point program created by Father Putz for Harvest House involves social awareness, service, new religious experiences, continuing education, celebration, and creativity. He stresses community involvement so that elders can unite to press for their economic rights in these years of devastating cuts for the elderly poor. They personally lobby legislators as well as write letters to fight cuts in Social Security, food stamps, Medicaid and Medicare. More than three times as many senior citizens vote as do the eighteen- and nineteen-year-old group enfranchised in the eighteen-year-old vote enacted in 1971. The number of seniors have increased from 22 million then to 27 million in 1983. The majority of the elders are women, since women outlive men. And the majority of them are without pensions or any other income to supplement their tiny Social Security check.

18. The Roman Catholic church officially sponsors its own peace and justice commissions and committees. Preceded by the long record of social action departments of mainstream Protestant churches, the increase in Roman Catholic groups has been accelerated not only by the threat of nuclear catastrophe but by our own bishops, who produced the peace pastoral The Challenge of Peace: God's Promise and Our Response, in May 1983. Peace and justice groups study other great renewal documents of the church as well. The group I took part in from 1982 to 1984 in Palm Beach county did more than study. Members conducted peace seminars, staffed a soup kitchen, The Lord's Place, in West Palm Beach, and did constant work on behalf of the migrants. We were lead by the Reverend Don Redden who learned liberation theology while practicing it in Peru.

19. Outstanding among the late-twentieth-century efforts for prayer and praxis are the thousands of basic Christian or ecclesial communities attached to the churches in Latin America, Africa, the British Isles, and the United States.[9]

Though there may be as many as three million women and men in the United States working in or actively reached by the above and other green-shoots groups, I would guess that we are still outnumbered twenty to one by those working for the kingdom of greed in our land. Many of the latter cling to a privatized, pietistic view of religion, and some of their leaders could even be called greedy-grabbers seeking the television audience dollars.

Before the reign of the religious and secular right, the United States experienced a period of ferment and reform from 1960 to 1972, both in the churches and in society. While Pope John XXIII and Vatican II opened to the modern world the Roman Catholic church, the election of John F. Kennedy in 1960 as president brought an influx of younger, more liberal men and women to Washington. More inportant, a revolution began in civil rights, followed by the women's movement revival in 1966.

When Martin Luther King, Jr. stood on the steps of the Lincoln Memorial in 1963 and exhorted 250,000 civil rights champions, "I have a dream," his call reached many millions who would join him in the struggle. When he was assassinated five years later, he died in continuity with the Judeo-Christian prophets and sidewalk contemplatives who have given their lives for their neighbors. Dr. King's nonviolent revolution for black equality brought white as well as black students into the civil rights movement. In 1960 Students for a Democratic Society was formed, calling not only for black dignity and equality but condemning war and anticommunism, attacking as dehumanizing and irresponsible the power of bureaucracies in government, corporations, universities, and labor unions. For a time, student strikes and takeovers on campuses got huge coverage in the media.

It took the Vietnam War, escalated under President Johnson, to turn the youth protest into the epochal, largely nonviolent movement that revealed the chasms dividing the nation on war and peace. The young men and women took to the streets in record numbers. In fact, one news item recently stated: "The greatest mass arrest reported in a democratic country took place in Washington, May 3–5, 1971, when police forced more than 13,000 people into custody during an anti-war demonstration...."[10] The young, by their massive protests, had already toppled President Johnson, causing him to abandon a reelection run in 1968.

The student antiwar movement, however, never quite took root as a force for radical social change. Instead, the young people began lacing their protest with drugs and booze, submerging themselves in the age of anesthesia from which those who did recover did so only to succumb to an addiction known as consumerism. They became the Yuppies of the 1980s. Their youthful visions were eclipsed by "making it." Reagan dismantled the college loan and other social programs that their parents' activism and dreams had made possible. Today "the people perish" as greater numbers than at any time since the 1930s Depression become ill fed, ill housed, and ill clothed. Today the nuclear clock ticks away at four minutes before midnight. Reagan's militarism runs riot around the world, blocking any chance to end the arms race.

We need sidewalk contemplatives deeply rooted in the love of God, saints for the common good who can work for the kingdom of God, the new society. Our century has not lacked models, as we have seen. And there are signs of hope in the green shoots under the nuclear mushroom: the steps toward unity among the churches— Catholic, Protestant, Eastern and Russian Orthodox, and Jews; in peace pilgrimages by the churches of the Soviet Union; in peace Pentecosts, and pledges of nonviolence. My dream is, of course, that we in the churches will also unite to invite all these forces to join in the One Day Buyers' Boycott already described. We could begin to launch a redemptive movement for the new society God plans for us.

Tools to Make Real the Vision
of the Best the World Can Be

1. Nourish your vision of the kingdom of God on earth by meditat-on the following Scripture: Isa. 10:20–23; 11:6–9; 35; 56:7; 33:15–20; 61:1–2; Jer. 31; Amos 9:13–15; Hos. 2:17–23; Joel 3:1–2; The Kingdom parables of Jesus, Matt. 13; and Luke 4:16–21; Matt. 11:2–6; Mark 4.

2. Love-bomb the present scene, i.e., transform, in vision, a corporate military state into a country of life and beauty-seeking saints-in-process, artists, and children.

3. Love-bomb a person, city, state, nation, and the world at this very moment.

4. Contrast your vision of the kingdom with what you are seeing daily in news accounts.

5. Read Leo Tolstoy's *The Kingdom of God Is Within You* (1893), Oxford Univ. Press, 1936, 1960 edition.

6. Practice step four of Breakthrough: We obtained a vision of the best the world could be, the kingdom of God, the new society that God plans for us.

7. Put protection of people and resources before exploitation in your daily life.

8. What have you done this week to increase the reign of the Divine Savior?

9. Put your action where your prayer is. Put your prayer where your action is.

BREAKTHROUGH STEP FIVE:
THE TURNING POINT

Step Five: We reached a turning point in which the old kingdom of greed battled with the emerging kingdom of God. Resistance to God is stubborn and violent.

Most of us are aliens in our own land; we have been exiled from our birthright—the kingdom of God, "the reign of truth and justice, the reign of peace and love." For the individual this alienation can be a dark night of the senses, even a dark night of the soul. St. John of the Cross, who wrote *The Dark Night of the Soul* in the sixteenth century, describes it in part: "But what the sorrowful soul feels most in this condition is its clear perception, as it thinks, that God has abandoned it, and, in His abhorrence of it, has flung it into darkness; . . . the soul feels very keenly the shadow of death and the lamentations of death and the pains of hell. . . . It feels, too, that all creatures have forsaken it, and that it is contemned by them, particularly by its friends."[1]

In our society the dark night is the "poisonous politics of the kingdom of darkness versus the kingdom of the light of God," said the Reverend Daniel Berrigan, S.J., addressing a community audience at St. Vincent de Paul Seminary, Boynton Beach, Florida, in 1985. "The preparations for the end of the world are not only legal, but 'religious.' The Pentagon is a vast religious shrine with the 'holy invocations' of the kingdom of Darkness—it involves idolatry of weaponry, demands the blood of children, and dwells within us demanding complete obedience." This kingdom of darkness is not only "larceny against the poor of the world, [it is] spiritual possession of the world by the demon of death. Death is causing despair. . . . Contempt for life is the most vicious and ruinous aim of the nuclear arms race."[2]

Dr. Robert J. Lifton, a Yale psychohistorian, calls the dark night that threatens a break with our very posterity. It is different from others in history because since 1945 humanity has had the capacity to destroy itself with the bomb. "The broken connection," as Dr. Lifton calls it, robs all of us, but especially the young, of a future. This alienation from our own posterity, he says, causes much of today's despair, unparalleled violence, and general disintegration.[3] Why work for a future or learn from the past if there is to be no future continuing after us?

When we confront ourselves and reflect in private on this dark night, we learn just how alienated we have become. Alienation takes three forms: spiritual, psychological, and social. We are, in fact, alienated from God, from ourselves, and from each other.

SPIRITUAL ALIENATION

The biblical basis for our spiritual alienation is told in the story of the Fall in Gen. 3:1–19. Since then we have been in the condition described by St. Paul: "For I do not do what I want, but I do the very thing I hate" (Rom. 7:15).

Erich Fromm wrote: "The disintegration of the love of God has reached the same proportions as the disintegration of the love of man."[4] And as quoted earlier, Professor Zaehner deplores ". . . the conversion of the American ideal of liberty into the most crassly materialist, soulless civilization the world has ever seen."[5]

When I take my nightly walks along the beach in my small seaside town, I see the flickering lights of the television through the unshaded windows of cottages and apartments. Heads can be seen glued to that Big Brother, the god of our time. The television has replaced the fireplace or the lamplight around which the family once gathered. Then there was conversation, some Bible reading, even singing to a banjo or an organ, that drew the family into a sharing circle. Some families even held hands for a good night prayer.

Today the television god preaches the gospel of greed for cars, cosmetics, drugs, and drink. Our near-total nightly silence is not the silence of thought, worship or prayer; it is the silence of dumb gaping, while we swallow the "word" as it is presented through script writers of soaps and/or ad writers for American business. Yet it is still true, I have found in my counseling practice, that, as Carl Jung once said, most people over the age of thirty-five are thirsting not for things, or for *spirits*, but for *Spirit*—God.

This craving for Spirit is seldom fed by the gospel Jesus preached. We have become so alienated from the *whole* gospel that we don't even recognize it when it is put into modern English. As we have seen, since the days of Constantine's conversion, early biblical Christianity was traded for state Christianity. The gospel became privatized into a conservative, individualistic, pietistic religiosity. The temporal and religious leaders agreed that it was far better to filter down to the masses a privatized interpretation of the Word of God, the deeds of God, and the concern of God for the poor. Gospel teaching and preaching became narrow and obscure, limited to tiny snippets read in Latin at Mass. Had our Lord returned to earth and dared to preach his whole gospel, the Grand Inquisitor would have burned him at the stake as a heretic, said Dostoevsky in *The Brothers Karamazov*.[6]

In the Roman Catholic church the faithful were discouraged from reading the Bible even when it finally became available in the vernacular after Martin Luther's reformation. It was a far too incendiary teaching, one that might incite to revolution the oppressed, hungry, restless Christians. Their rulers—secular and religious—didn't want peasants and the urban poor to read such texts: "Is it not the rich who oppress you, is it not they who drag you into court? Is it not they who blaspheme that honorable name by which you are called?" (James 2:6–7); or "A man murders his neighbor if he robs him of his livelihood, sheds blood if he withholds an employee's wages" (Ecclus. 34:22).

In our day Protestant theologian Frederick Herzog writes: "Christianity needs to own up to its very own revolutionary dynamic. Where divine justice is not embodied by the church, people outside the church take matters into their own hands. This is the story of Karl Marx."[7]

I was exposed to the "revolutionary dynamic" of the Protestant church when I was nineteen years old through five southern Christian young ladies. They also happened to be radically committed to social change. We worked together for the American Friends Service Committee in what was called the Emergency Peace campaign. We were sent to Augusta, Georgia. A score or more of teams were sent (like the civil rights youth of the 1960s) to other parts of the South and even to the Midwest.

Their enthusiastic activism for peace was one of the contributing factors in my lifetime search for radical social change. In fact, their political stance was a far more potent attraction to one of my heritage than their low-key Christian witness. Back at college in the North, I was lionized by the secular center and left because of my name and energy. I never even heard God alluded to on campus except during folk-song festivals or old union songs that mocked the "pie in the sky when you die" offered by capitalists in lieu of living wages on earth.

It was not until I became a convert that I began to look for the "revolutionary dynamic" in Christianity. But by then as a captive of the cold war I was barred from any and all political expression. So my delighted discovery of the *whole* gospel of Jesus had to take place when I was forced to live in burning silence. I could share my views with only a few Catholic friends and teachers. But I could nourish my new radical Christian education not only with the gospel but with the documents of the church moving into the modern world through Vatican II.

Meanwhile, the prophets were still being killed—both the Hindu Gandhi and the Christian Martin Luther King, Jr., the geniuses of nonviolent revolutionary change. The poet of peace, John Lennon, was gunned down by a Fundamentalist extremist. Allard Lowenstein, a peace and justice prophet, was assassinated as his desk in the prime of life. Other prophets were silenced through deportation, jail sentences (i.e., the Berrigan brothers) and poverty-induced malnutrition, illness, and work-induced exhaustion.

Robbed of prophets, the masses of people in our country have become sheep without shepherds, pathetic moral delinquents, violent murderers, rapists, drug and alcohol abusers. Watergate showed the extent of wickedness in high places. Biblical justice has been ignored at every level of national and international action since the most immoral act of all, the large-scale killing of civilians at Hiroshima and Nagasaki.

We have become so alienated from our spiritual center that we not only fail to consult our conscience, we even blot out the instinct of self-preservation, generally thought to be ineradicable. Contempt for life bred by the dogma of the national nuclear state has led us to the fatalistic acceptance of genocide, past and present; to soaring civilian homicides and to mass suicide (Jonestown). We rob ourselves and our children of adequate food, medical care, housing, and education to support the nuclear arms race. We have even been sold by our leaders into a perverted kind of pride that our nation is rich enough in manpower and weapons to throw away in Vietnam the lives of 58,000 young Americans, not to mention the hundreds of thousands left wounded and mentally maimed. This is aside from the irreversible damage done to our economy and destabilization of our democratic institutions.

Our spiritual alienation is shown also by a world willingness to replace the worship of a supernatural or infinite person or power with that of secular messiahs. Military dictatorships and even a national security state such as ours have put the religion of nuclear supremacy above the God of Abraham, Isaac and Jacob, and his Son, Jesus Christ. For the spiritually alienated it is a kind of relief to be able to put all trust in a Big Brother. Let him take away anxiety, choice, responsibility. The human messiah—whether fascist or communist—asserts his God-like power to heal or to kill. Men and women will lie, cheat, subvert elections, torture, and murder at his command. Their spiritual alienation, however, must be reinforced by psychological alienation if the total disintegration of the independent thinking person is to be attained. Men and women must be trained to ignore the ancient stern and holy warning: "Put not your trust in men in power, in any mortal man—he cannot save" (Ps. 146:3).

PSYCHOLOGICAL ALIENATION

The disintegration of the love of man has reached the same proportion as the disintegration of the love of God. This is a transposition of Erich Fromm's quote used earlier in this chapter. In fact, psychological alienation could be described as consciousness disintegration. It manifests in our soaring statistics on substance abuse, mental illness, divorce, delinquency, and violence. The breakdown of the individual psyche is matched by the breakdown in the endemic fear and hate of our time. I have isolated what I call the "Seven D's of Disintegration" that dominate the dark night of the soul in our society as well as in the self. They are distract, divert, disorient, divide, disrupt, depersonalize, and destroy.

Now I don't claim to see any evil genius sitting in his think tank and asking what are the most effective techniques of consciousness disintegration. Rather, I think that techniques take over as cause and effect when we choose the kingdom of greed rather than the kingdom of God. Psychological alienation separates us from ourselves and our neighbors. We not only blot out our personal suffering or insight, we alienate ourselves from the collective unconscious of the human race. In so doing, we also become alienated from the saving love and redemption of Jesus, which some Jungians say reside in the collective unconscious.

A result is that "our highest goal . . . is to be free of suffering, to become free of it and remain free of it right up to the moment of death" writes Dorothee Soelle.[8] She quotes Leszek Kolakowski:

"One of the most important though rarely articulated characteristics of our civilization is the total rejection of belief in the value of suffering." Our society, he says, is a "culture of analgesics" in which there is a "headlong flight from suffering," a "narcotizing of life."[9] Yet, he continues, "The narcotizing of life is the enemy of human community. The more incapable we become of bearing our own suffering the easier it becomes for us to ignore the suffering of others...."[10]

Alcohol is the drug of choice in the United States because it is both legal and cheap compared with heroin and cocaine. More than one-quarter of the entire U.S. population, or more than 56 million persons, drink. At least 15 million are alcoholics. Drug abusers have soared three to five million in the current cocaine epidemic. Drugs and alcohol combined comprise one of the main tools of consciousness disintegration—they distract, divert, disorient, divide, disrupt, depersonalize, and destroy. While substance abuse demands the voluntary act of taking a drink or a drug, other forms of psychological alienation are involuntary. They include feelings of self-rejection —most apparent in the First World. As Fromm says, the economic and social structure of Western civilization cause people to be viewed as things, rather than persons. We are regarded as commodities by the big institutions and corporations of the postindustrial world. Remember the human "canaries" Union Carbide allegedly used at their West Virginia plant to test the air for lethal pollution?

Perhaps our feeling of being things, not persons, explains in part the phenomenal growth of self-help groups copying the twelve steps of Alcoholics Anonymous. At least they can feel like persons rather than things when sharing their suffering with others.

Veterans of the Vietnam War, trained to view the enemy as less than human, are finally getting help in group sharing—sharing of the nonfeelings they once admitted to as they plunged a bayonet into the living, breathing enemy. "It was not a person I was killing. It was a thing," said one verteran. Before the soldiers could depersonalize their victims, they themselves had to become alienated.

Alas, they exemplify what we are all being conditioned to become—slaughterers of millions of innocent people in a nuclear war.

Only a minority of those who are psychologically alienated can afford the money and time to get psychotherapy. There they face the danger of prescription drugs, mood changers that might blur the too devastating insights. Addiction often results from perfectly innocent ingestion. Others may be told that they must learn to adjust to society as it is. This hardly seems to be a solution, since it may be that society has helped alienate the patient in the first place.

SOCIAL ALIENATION

The battle of the kingdom of greed versus the kingdom of God shows its darkest aspects in social alienation. Karl Marx used the word alienation more than 100 years ago to describe modern man's alienation from the means of production. Today the term has been broadened to include the technique of divide and rule. The oldest divisions are sexism, classism, and racism. In 1975 our Applachian Catholic bishops wrote:

> *The people had to fight one another*
> *for the few jobs:*
>
> *—mountain people against city people,*
> *—white people against black people,*
> *—Irish people against Polish and Italian people,*
> *—skilled workers against unskilled workers,*
> *—union workers against nonunion workers . . .*
>
> *But many people stayed poor,*
> *and suffered attacks on their dignity,*
> *especially*
>
> *—Indians,*
> *—blacks,*

—*Mexican Americans,*
—*immigrants,*
—*Puerto Ricans,*
—*and poor whites, like Appalachians.*

Brothers and sisters in suffering,
These people were often forced
to turn against one another,
for some meager piece of a pie,
which, however big,
(the biggest the world had ever known),
refused to feed all its children. [11]

Divide and rule is the first commandment in the consciously and constantly maintained economic alienation of the poor. The first alienation experienced by the masses of people in the world was their separation from the land; the second their separation from the means of production, while the alienations mentioned by the bishops above were continued.

Divide and rule was injected to break up the civil rights movement during the sixties. Dr. King held it together through sheer spiritual force and brilliance. But after his death the agents provocateurs began to split the movement, all but destroying its effectiveness.

The Reverend Jesse Jackson and Dr. King's widow, Coretta Scott King—together with hundreds of labor, church, and black and ethnic leaders—are trying once more to unite the elements that won civil rights for blacks. Now their goals have been broadened to include jobs and peace. Any such coalition has be contend with the long and bitter competition for "some meager piece of a pie." Nor is this competition accidental. It is maintained by the propaganda of alienation. Will Campbell, writing about the South, says the gentry perfected the technique of dividing the poor whites from the poor blacks to keep both fighting for the meager earnings. He said to both blacks and whites, "Don't let them take your head away from you." The Appalachian bishops wrote: ". . . it has become clear to us that the present economic order does not care for its people . In fact, profit and people frequently are contradictory. Profit over people is an idol. And it is not a new idol, for Jesus long ago warned us, 'No one can serve two masters: . . . Ye cannot serve God and mammon'" (Matt. 6:24).[12]

Even the oppressed peasants of czarist Russia could be turned against each other when their masters commanded. Leo Tolstoy describes how the czar's police descended upon a village and forced whips into the hands of the peasants. Then they ordered the peasants to flog each other. Stupefied by years of unthinking obedience, the peasants stripped the raw flesh off each other in a frenzy of fear.

Count Tolstoy used this story in his peace writings to illustrate that warmakers who fan divisions among the populace are like the czarist rulers.[13] If we were not alienated from each other we could not conceive of killing each other. Instead, however, we are constantly given the whip of competition, of climbing upward on the backs of our neighbors. We are taught to hate especially the scapegoats, Communists, Jews, blacks, youths, and women. The scapegoat becomes the projection for one's own self-hate as person, nation, class, race. The scapegoat is the object of harassment, jailing, concentration camps, and execution. During the first half of the twentieth century the leading scapegoats were the Jews, who were blamed by Hitler for Germany's problems, and then exterminated. Not satisfied with killing "only" the German Jews, Hitler denationalized Europe's Jews so they would have no nation to protect them, and then began their systematic extermination.

In the United States, as we have seen, there is a far less violent but equally deadly future (in the long run) for the poor. The need for workers in manufacturing industries and on farms has declined in the postindustrial age. Why give health care to those who are no longer needed to settle, farm, build and make things in this receding economy? They are expendable. A high proportion of draftees for the Vietnam bloodbath consisted of poor blacks and poor whites. A kind of civilian extermination began in 1981 with the cuts in life-saving programs to feed, medically care for and house the poor of all races, ages, and both sexes. Our country was settled and built upon the extermination of the Native Americans as a nation. It fattened on the slave labor of the blacks, who were valuable property to their owners and, after emancipation, valuable competitors with the poor whites. If Martin Luther King, Jr.'s liberation efforts had remained limited to blacks only, instead of extending to whites in planned poor peoples' crusades, he might not have been assassinated.

The day after his death I came home from Marymount College where I was teaching (our college president had dismissed all classes in honor of his memory) to find a sleek new Cadillac drawing up to my front yard. A white matron with blue hair knocked on my door. She asked me rather imperiously if I would talk to her about her alcoholic daughter. I said, of course, but later. First I must take time to pray myself out of shock at Dr. King's assassination. She strode off toward her car in a huff, flinging out loud and clear, "What a blessing that man has been killed. Now there'll be no more of that awful trouble he's been stirring up with the nigras."

Many of us have had our turn as scapegoats—women, union members, those of us who were unfriendly to or refused to testify in the McCarthy hearings. The perennial scapegoats year in and year out are the liberal to left activists. Called anarchists, Communists, or liberals, depending upon which term is in greatest disrepute, the left has been punished as a handy scapegoat for terrorism, riots, boycotts, depressions, inflation—any unpopular condition.

Hidden in history today lest they inspire the young to champion unpopular causes are labor leaders and others who were hanged after they were convicted for bombings that most fair jurists say they never did. If you want to find honor given in death to a labor leader, such as "Big" Bill Haywood of the Industrial Workers of the World, you will have to go to the Kremlin wall, where he and John Reed are buried. Hidden in history also are Sacco and Vanzetti, and the leaders of the unemployed and veteran marchers on Washington during the Depression, or the militant organizers of the CIO during the 1930s, who won a union despite the violence used against them.

Since the onset of the nuclear state inauguarated by Hiroshima, many liberals have been lumped with leftists under the most hated word of all, "Communist." A two-bit politician or scurrilous newsletter has only to cry "Communist," and the full force of the U.S. government is invoked to cripple that person's freedom—economic, social, and political.

The Allies won the war against Hitler but lost the peace. The techniques of discrimination against political, racial, and religious minorities, that we fought to destroy in Nazism and Fascism, have become part of the doctrine—open or veiled—of the religious right as well as the secular state. Yet most of us practice what Dr. King called "the betrayal of silence." We are like the "good" German who said: "I didn't speak out when the Nazis killed the Communists. I didn't speak out when the Nazis killed the Jews. Now that the Nazis have also killed the Catholics, there is no one left to speak out."

Economic alienation of the people from ownership of their land and from the means of production had been largely achieved by World War I. Social alienation only began in earnest, however, with Mussolini's Fascist takeover in Italy immediately after World War I. Since then totalitarianism and terrorism of the right have spread around the world like a deadly radioactive cloud.

Fascist Italy was followed by Fascist Japan, and Nazi Germany to form the Axis; by Fascist Spain, and the following Fascist takeovers: Argentina, Brazil, El Salvador, Chiang Kai-Shek's China, Iran, Chile, and others. Totalitarianism of the left in the Societ Union, China, and smaller Eastern bloc countries distinguishes itself from that of the right. It aims to serve the poor and oppressed in socialist states based on production for use, not profit. The Nazis and Fascists never tried to conceal the fact that they were financed by the giant corporations in their war on the poor and the left.

The loss of human freedom is the same in both totalitarianism of right and left, according to most politicians. But having toured, even briefly, Naxi Germany as a college student and Soviet Russia twice as a mature woman, I would say that tourists, at least, are far freer in the various republics of the Soviet Union now than in the past. I could wander alone anywhere I chose; I could chat with Soviets on the street, or in stores or restaurants. I could and did attend scores of churches from Leningrad to Yerevan when I chose. I was also free of the midnight search the Nazi police had made of my room, luggage, and me in 1938.

Here at home there has been no violent overthrow of our constitutional form of government by right- or left-wing totalitarian dictators. Here the alienation of our people from their economic, social, and political rights has been so gradual that few have noticed it. I call it the "creeping conglomerate conspiracy." It has conspired to seize absolute control of the world's wealth, beginning with the United States. These multinational giants and their lobbyists decree, without our having to cast a single vote for them, what you and I eat, drink, pay, live in, study, wear. Our Congress, though elected (by a dwindling proportion of the people), has become nonrepresentative of even the flabby will of the people—increasingly becoming a copy of the Reichstag under Hitler.

The Appalachian bishops had prophesied: "Unaccountable economic powers will continue to use democratic political institutions for nondemocratic purposes. Sometimes this shows itself brutally when policemen act like company enforcers. At other times it is more complicated, when lawyers and legislators seem to get paid to keep the people confused, and to find loopholes for the benefit of the rich. These same massive economic forces, still accountable to no one, will even use the vehicles of our cultural life, like communications media and advertising, and even the educational system, to justify their ways and to pass off their values as our national values. This happens when news that's important to people can't get time or space, or when school programs are designed by experts without incorporating the voice of the people."[14]

This prophetic statement made by the bishops in 1975 has alas been made more manifest in the Reagan administration. Multinational interest groups are getting their freest ride in the history of the republic. They control not only Congress but much of the entire government bureaucracy. Their virtual control of many state legislatures and state houses is well known. One could call the Reagan era a "welfare state for the rich." Meanwhile the poor, whose care programs have been abolished or stripped to the bone, are dying faster. Infant mortality rates have gone up. The aged get discharged while still ill, it is reported, due to cuts in Medicare. The United States ranks lowest among industrialized nations in services for families, especially medical and child care.

Since 1940 I have followed the fate of preschool and after-school day-care projects for the children of working mothers. Federal funding entered the picture during WPA days when some model day-care centers were set up. Just as they were about to be wiped out due to lack of funding, World War II brought them back for the duration only. Since then not even the minimum bill for day care, enacted by Congress in 1971 but vetoed by Nixon, has been legislated. We have cut maternal aid programs; Aid to families of dependent children (more than 90 percent of such families are headed by women) has been curtailed by provisos forcing mothers of children over six years out to work despite the fact that there is no federal or any other universal system of day-care facilities for children. The feminization of poverty has reached massive proportions. "Two out of every three poor adults in this country are women." [15]

We have seen how privatizing the gospel delayed the church from declaring its "preferential option for the poor" until 1968. Privatizing services not only for the poor but for the entire community threatens to regress us to the nineteenth century, when the public was left to the untender charity doled out by the rich. During the 1980s private industry has been allowed the largest maximization of profits in peacetime since before World War I. At the same time, the poor have been deprived services they have had since the Roosevelt administration tried to end the Great Depression. While Hitler singled out the Jews more than any other group for his special targets, Reagan's programs have brought suffering to all the poor without regard for race, religion, sex, age, or ethnic background.

Our homeless—many of them women, some of them mentally ill—

who have been put out on the street because of the shutdown of state-supported mental hospitals, wander in hunger, cold, and filth for want of safe shelter. The homeless are victimized as well as ignored. They are evicted even from the steam grates outside the dormitories of Harvard University. The women tried to find some warmth but instead got evicted, then barred from the steam grates by the erection of barbed wire. Protest forced Harvard to remove the barbed wire. But they did not, of course, remove the problem.

Meanwhile, war contractors win millions of dollars for our military excursions into Third World countries such as Grenada, Honduras as well as El Salvador, the *contra* war against Nicaragua, and the bombing of Libya. The Appalachian bishops deplored the "unaccountable enonomic powers." Congress had actually preceded the executive branch and its commander in chief in undemocratic actions. As far back as 1938 it voted for and funded the notorious U.S. House Un-American Activities Committee, first under Martin Dies. One of the committee's first actions was to whip up hysteria to pass the Smith Act, making illegal what has always been legal in a democratic country—the Communist party. The officers of the Party were carted off to jail to serve time for violation of the Smith Act, for allegedly seeking the violent overthrow of the U.S. government.

In Montgomery, Alabama, meanwhile, two incidents occurred that would alter the course of black history in America. In 1955 Mrs. Rosa Parks refused to go to the back of the bus as blacks had historically done without question. A major result of this act of courage was the year-long boycott of the Montgomery bus system led by young Martin Luther King, Jr. It ended in victory on November 1956, when the Supreme Court ruled segregation on buses to be unconstitutional. This marked the beginning of a nonviolent revolution, patterned, Dr. King said, on the women's suffrage movement. The miracle of civil disobedience, rooted in prayer, of the largely religious leadership of the black movement, made sidewalk contemplatives not only of blacks but of white clergy, rabbis and the concerned everywhere.

In 1966 women began to rattle their chains as they attempted to finish the work started by the nineteenth-century suffrage pioneers. Though the renewed movement has made strides for women, so far it has failed to link up effectively with those trying to combat the feminization of poverty—the major problem facing American women and their children today.

Many saw the young people as the hope of the future. But we have seen that the militant students who took part in the massive demonstrations against the Vietnam War never fulfilled their promise. Instead they reverted to the middle-class goals of upward mobility. Their drugged and drunken disintegration deterred *conscientization* of the young even further.

One might say the fifties was the decade of the blacks; the sixties of the black and the young, and the seventies of women's consciousness raising. The 1980s have become the decade of the churches. The religious left is the brightest light in a darkening century. Vatican II brought the church into the modern world and stimulated the declaration by Latin American bishops of a "preferential option for the poor." Canadian bishops followed our Appalachian bishops in 1977 with their own challenging statement in 1983: "We need economic policies which realize that the needs of the poor have priority over the wants of the rich; that the rights of workers are more important than the maximization of profits."[16]

But it was out of the barrios and stricken rural areas of Latin America that the formulation of liberation theology came to enlighten the entire church—Catholic, Protestant, and Orthodox. *Conscientization* of the poor in base communities attached to churches has been the soil in which liberation theology has grown. It has sent forth its green shoots to the entire believing world. It is the brightest and most hopeful sign, I think, for these last years of the twentieth century. Girded by the gospel of the kingdom of God on earth as it is in heaven, liberation theologians can and do battle against the old kingdom of greed. We can even confront the detractors and opponents within our own house of prayer—whatever the church—and expose the greedy-grabbers who seek to make our world a "den of thieves."

Thanks to liberation theology there is a place in some churches today for witnessing to our own oppression—whether as the poor, blacks, women, Appalachians, Hispanics, Native Americans. Sharing our hurts, we gain a new consciousness and a new strength, and, above all, a new solidarity with which we can deal with the hurt. Gustavo Gutierrez, father of liberation theology says: "All the political theologies, the theologies of hope, of revolution, and of liberation, are not worth one act of genuine solidarity with exploited social classes."[17] I would add that solidary action with our brothers and sisters must be rooted in solitary contemplation, and that means surrendering myself to God.

Tools to Win the Battle
of the Kingdom of God
Versus the Kingdom of Greed

1. ". . . and you will know the truth, and the truth will make you free" (John 8:32). Strip yourself of your present stupor about the world. Break through the age of anesthesia.
2. Develop and ponder your vision of the new society—the kingdom of God.
3. Immerse yourself in the gospel to offset any alienation from Jesus.
4. Pray and act to deliver the systems—political, economic, religious —from their bondage to evil. Study liberation theology.
5. Repeat daily for the hungry: "Give us this day our daily bread."
6. Practice gratitude. You have survived till this moment!
7. For perspective on the past and present, reread the first 823 pages of William Shirer's *The Rise and Fall of the Third Reich.*
8. Develop your perspective on the present—a sense of humor. Remember, "A cheerful heart is a good medicine, but a downcast spirit dries up the bones" (Prov. 17:22). Dilute the dark night with humor. Try laughing at the madness of the world as it is. Read and see some good satires on the madness—such as *The Gods Must Be Crazy, Dr. Strangelove or: How I Learned to Stop Worrying and Love the Bomb, The Bridge on the River Kwai, It's a Mad, Mad, Mad, Mad World,* and others.
9. Read Norman Cousins's *Anatomy of an Illness,* Chapter 1.

SEVEN.

Breakthrough Step Six:
SURRENDER

Step Six: We surrendered to the reign of God in our lives—personally and socially—practicing obedience to God moment by moment.

We can only begin to surrender to Jesus and his socializing gospel of the kingdom if we are at least personally trying to surrender to his spiritualizing gospel. In my book *Survival Kit* I wrote this step for personal surrender only: "We surrendered ourselves to God, moment by moment, seeking the state of abandonment to God as a way of life."[1] Among the biblical sources for personal surrender are Matt. 6:10 and 26:39; and Gal. 2:20. Personal surrender is the road to freedom from self. When the Holy Spirit gave me my first prayer poem a year after I had met Jesus as Lord, it was to help me in my efforts to attain freedom from self. The first line that came to me was, "Lord, empty me of me."

Fifteen years earlier I had taken the primary step toward personal surrender in step one of Breakthrough to the new self: "We admitted we were powerless over our suffering and/or the particular defect that is keeping us from making a breakthrough from what we are to what God wants us to be, and that only God can help us to survive." I began to surrender my major defect, alcoholism, first through sharing and later through prayer and sharing. But I couldn't seem to surrender my self-will; I couldn't even attempt to give up my self-concern. I was still, as Evelyn Underhill says, "coiled tightly around myself"—the very opposite of "a person completely redeemed from self-occupation."[2]

On the eve of my conversion to Jesus as Lord I had been given the grace of an instruction on surrender that would carry me through when I needed it. This technique was handed down from Father Jean-Pierre de Caussade, an eighteenth-century Jesuit, in his classic, *Self-Abandonment to Divine Providence.* I pored over his words as I flew west, unknowingly to my conversion, in 1960.

He wrote that I did not have to make a sweeping, all-inclusive lifetime surrender to God. I could, if that were too difficult, surrender *this* moment only. He called this the "sacrament of the present moment." It is not necessary to surrender tomorrow or next year, but just this moment, he said. Nor is it necessary to know the will of God for tomorrow. It is only necessary to accept, to abandon yourself to God's will as it unfolds in your life *moment by moment.*[3] Whether it is a letter of rejection, the diagnosis of an illness, the loss of a job, a triumph or a suffering, what this moment brings is God's will for you. Personal surrender is the sovereign way out of a dark night, and it can come as a gift or through ardent prayer, meditation and sharing, or through models.

Frances and Richard Hadden, the celebrated duo-pianists, have for twenty years provided models of surrender for me when I most needed them. Known to the world for decades as master musicians, and to Christians as a unique husband and wife team in their marriage as well as their music, the Haddens have alternated between the cross and the crown. They have played for twenty-six heads of state; and at the invitation of Premier Chou En-lai they became in 1972 the first American artists to perform in China since the People's Republic of China was established in 1949. Born in China, Frances is the daughter of the late bishop of Hank'ou, Logan Herbert Roots. As a young woman she was a close family friend of Generalissimo and Madame Chiang Kai-shek, who followed her career with great interest.

Moved by the Spirit, the Haddens interrupted a thirty-four-year international musical ministry to head the music department of a new and unique nondenominational liberal arts college on Mackinac Island in the sixties. Generously, they donated a large portion of their salaries to the nonendowed college to help keep it going. But it closed, leaving the Haddens broke. They took to the Lord, surrendering to him this economic disaster, and bounced back with a seven-week tour of China as Prime Minister Chou's guests. Returning in triumph, they gave a command performance at the White House, a concert at Town Hall, and an appearance on the *Today* show with Barbara Walters. They were "on the road" once more. They conceived and had built a motor home large enough for their two seven-foot Baldwin grand pianos, and sleeping and living quarters for themselves. Freed from the expense of hotels along the highways, they drive the mobile studio from California to Florida to New England on their annual tours. They have traveled 165,000 miles in it and are now entering their sixteenth season of continuous concertizing across America.

They were on tour in New Jersey in April 1986 when a phone call informed them that Frances Hadden's brother Sheldon and sister Elizabeth, both in their mid-seventies, had just been killed in a propane explosion and fire that had completely destroyed the Haddens' home and studio on Mackinac Island, Michigan. Everything they had in the world—their practice pianos, extensive libraries and files on all subjects, music and book manuscripts, photographs and memorabilia—every bit of clothing—was destroyed.

My longtime friend and Mackinac Island hostess since 1963, Hope Goodwin, called me that day with the news. I pulled from my bookcase *The Will of God* by Leslie Weatherhead after reading the Office for the Dead in my prayer book. I knew, and I knew that the Haddens would realize instantly, that it was *not* the intentional will of God to let their beloved siblings perish by fire and to strip them of all but the concert clothes and the concert pianos they had on tour.

When I reached them by phone at their temporary quarters at the island's vicarage, they both got on the phone. Their voices sounded not flat but triumphant with love and gratitude at what their friends and neighbors were doing for them; and how the memory of Sheldon's and Beth's faith-filled lives was already beginning to heal a number of longtime feuds on the island. I could tell that they were letting this bitterest of all cups pass from them. They were wasting no time in lamenting "Why us?" They were already planning where they would put their grand pianos for practicing and, more important, they were searching God's mind for their next steps into the future. I could only admire their surrender, not to the circumstances, but to God.

When my own dark night, my captivity during the cold war, overshadowed my life, I realized that I should view it as a test of my real, not imagined, readiness for self-abandonment to Divine Providence as the Haddens practice it, and as Father de Caussade taught it. Instead, I argued constantly with God. Surrender doesn't mean giving up and going into permanent exile. It couldn't! After all, I had committed no crime, no sin even. I had simply championed unpopular causes for the poor. I lived on a constant seesaw between determination to succeed in my legal battle with the Immigration and Naturalization Service and letting go and letting God.

All hope was fading. As mentioned earlier, we appealed to the court of last resort, the U.S. Board of Immigration Appeals. My friends mounted a prayer vigil nationwide on my behalf. I became very busy getting letters out to prayer groups and individuals around the country (with much help from my students and prayer partners). I didn't realize at the time that I was giving less and less thought each day to myself and more to gratitude for the prayer and work of my friends.

Even so I would dip into a depression as the days turned into weeks with no reprieve handed down by the Board. The day came when I couldn't work at my typewriter, or even pay bills, I was so uneasy. What I finally did was find a prayer partner, Faith Smith, to carry me through that day. Together we prayed on the beach, while walking, or at lunch. We prayed for my complete surrender. On the way home, quite illogically, I thought, the phrase came to me: "Enter his gates with thanksgiving and his courts with praise!"

(Ps. 100) Back home I picked up a Bible and read it over and over again. On my nightly walk along the sea I said the verse under the dark sky repeatedly and returned home to sleep deeply for the first time in weeks.

The next morning the sun shone. It shone even brighter when Grover Cleveland Herring, my hardworking lawyer, had me called with the good news that I was free at last. All deportation proceedings had been dropped! I was as American as apple pie. Mountains of prayer, plus my belated self-abandonment to Divine Providence, as Father de Caussade suggested, had opened the doors to freedom. I was learning that the ultimate freedom *from* self can be obtained through the ultimate surrender *of* self. A further step is needed for *social* surrender—surrender to the kingdom of God, the common good. Social surrender is the opposite of the "me first"—*my* private good first, *my* profits, *my* ambitions—inculcated by the kingdom of greed discussed in the preceding chapter. When one surrenders to the prophetic imagination, one is redeemed from self-occupation or self-obsession.

The good news is that examples of surrender to the kingdom of God on earth have been increasing since Jesus showed the way of nonviolence. He sent forth his Apostles armed with the Word, not the sword, to be his witnesses "to the end of the earth" (Acts 1:8).

The early Christian missionaries spilled no blood but their own. They paid the martyrs' price by the thousands while gaining the Christianization of hundreds of thousands in the Mediterranean world. The martyrology of the early Christian church is an epic of social surrender, the surrender of nonviolent resistance. They held on to their Christian beliefs while letting go of their lives for the highest good of the universe—God.

The nonviolent roots of the gospel and the apostolic era were obscured and diminished by the "victories" of Satan, according to Professor Zaehner. They included: "The conversion of Constantine which subjected the Eastern Church to the imperial power; the spurious Donation of Constantine which made the Papacy itself a temporal power . . . the dissensions and corruption of medieval

Christendom; the religious wars of the sixteenth and seventeenth centuries...."⁴

But in each century there were those who championed a nonviolence that crossed the Atlantic with the Quakers to the colonies and bred the holy John Woolman. He not only lived the Quaker life of simplicity, prayer and nonviolence, he taught it. He was years ahead of his time, even for a Quaker, in preaching abolition of slavery to the slave owners among his own Quaker brethren. Lucretia Mott, the Philadelphia Quaker, and the Grimke sisters, former slave owners from the South, followed in his abolitionist advocacy. Lucretia was to make nonviolence a cornerstone of the new women's movement that burst upon the country at Seneca Falls, New York, in 1848 (the first women's rights convention in the world). She and the cosigners of "The Declaration of the Rights of Women," including my great-grandparents and great-aunt, Mary Anthony (Susan was off teaching school in the eastern part of the state) didn't realize that Susan and Lucretia and Elizabeth would lead the longest nonviolent struggle for social change in U.S. history—seventy-two years.

Susan pioneered in carrying out the first nonviolent civil disobedience for women in 1872, twenty-six years after Henry David Thoreau got himself jailed in protest against slavery by refusing to pay his poll tax. Susan gathered fifteen Rochester, New York, housewives, overwhelmed the election inspectors by her eloquence, and had themselves arrested for voting "illegally." Alas her lawyer paid her $100 fine, much against her will, barring her way to jail and the Supreme Court. But her highly publicized trial gave the women's movement the national coverage they desired. The press even publicized the Sixteenth Amendment, which Aunt Susan had gotten introduced in Congress. It would not pass, of course, until it became the Nineteenth Amendment in 1920, fourteen years after her death.

Martin Luther King, Jr. traced his own epic strategy of nonviolence for black civil rights back to the women's civil rights movement from 1848 to 1920. He wrote that women "were far from submissive or silent. They cried out in the halls of government....

They protested in the streets. And they were jailed. From these women we have learned how social change take place through struggle. In this same tradition of determination, of confidence in the justice of a cause, Negroes must now demand the right to vote. And these qualities of courage, perseverance, unity, sacrifice, plus a nonviolence of spirit, are the weapons we must depend upon if we are to vote with freedom."[5] Later he wrote: ". . . I came to see . . . that the Christian doctrine of love operating through the Gandhian method of nonviolence was one of the most potent weapons available to oppressed people in their struggle for freedom."[6]

In accepting the leadership of the Montgomery, Alabama, bus boycott for desegregation in 1956, Dr. King wrote: "My mind consciously or unconsciously was driven back to the Sermon on the Mount and the Gandhian method of nonviolent resistance. Christ furnished the spirit and motivation while Gandhi furnished the method."[7] Following in the footsteps of Jesus and of Gandhi, Dr. King paid the ultimate price—martyrdom for his nonviolent revolution that led *From Montgomery to Memphis*, as the great documentary film is called. No one who heard his voice, or saw, even on film, the nonviolent resistance at the Selma, Alabama, bridge with armed police and police dogs attacking kneeling, praying blacks and whites will ever forget that "we shall overcome." The editor of Dr. King's extensive published papers says in the introduction to his book in 1986:

> He was indeed a world historical figure. He captured the spotlight of history precisely at the right time, and responded with a blueprint for what America could become if it trusted its democratic legacy. His dreams proved to be too threatening. He was murdered. But his dream still excites our social and political imaginations . . . that America can indeed be a . . . place in the universe where peace, justice and freedom are the dominant ethos.[8]

Dorothy Day, whose work preceded Dr. King's by more than twenty years, was a pioneer in the Roman Catholic church in her consistent civil disobedience. She began as a young feminist arrested in the women's suffrage picket line around the White House (1917–1919). She was carried off to Occoquan workhouse with 267 other suffrage picketers, went on a ten-day hunger strike with some of them, and, like others, was manhandled by prison guards. Forty years later she was still championing the doctrine of nonviolence and those who practiced it. Addressing a rally for the Berrigan brothers, who were arrested for pouring blood on draft files in protest against the Vietnam War, she said:

"I've been in jail for civil disobedience more often than any of you, and I know more clearly than any of you the courage it entails . . . and I know that we must hang on to our pacifism . . . the way Gandhi, Martin Luther King, and Cesar Chavez retained it; it's the most difficult thing in the world, and the one that requires most faith."

Earlier she had said: "I came here to express my sympathy for this act of nonviolent revolution, for this act of peaceful sabotage which is not only a revolution against the state but against the alliance of Church and state, an alliance which has gone on much too long . . . only actions such as these will force the Church to speak out when the state has become a murderer. The act of the Catonsville nine is another desperate offer of life and freedom. But, my friends, we must restrict our violence to property. . . ."[9]

True to her beliefs and practice, Dorothy Day continued her nonviolent civil disobedience throughout the years of her life following her conversion to the Roman Catholic church in 1927. She founded the *Catholic Worker* newspaper with Peter Maurin on May Day, 1933. She continued her work for the poor and oppressed, and for peace, even in her eighties. One of the most widely printed news photos could be seen around the world. It shows Dorothy in jail at seventy-six, perched on a tiny shooting stick, photographed by an intrepid newsperson who filmed her between the widespread, uniformed legs of a burly sheriff's officer or policeman holding a club. It was 1973, and she and about 1,000 others had been arrested for demonstrating with the United Farm Workers Union in the San Joaquin Valley in California.

I had the great honor of interviewing Dorothy Day in 1975 (five years before her death) at the Lower East Side Catholic Worker house that continues to provide the hungry daily with food. It has also fed—socially and spiritually—a wide assortment of people for more than fifty years, through weekly lectures and the *Catholic Worker* newspaper. She is the closest I have come to meeting face-to-face a saint for the common good—the essence of personal surrender to Jesus, and social surrender to his kingdom on earth. She cared for the immediate needs of the individual poor, as have so many since Christ. But she also sought to change the social structures that rob and kill the poor everywhere in the world.

She who was so frequently in jail for her beliefs and actions would be proud today that there are more religious and lay persons in jail or awaiting sentence to jail than at any time in our history. They were arrested and sentenced for antinuclear actions, draft resistance, or for giving sanctuary to desperate Central American refugees fleeing for their lives across the border with the help of church persons.

The Reverend Douglas Roth, thirty-four, fought not only for his own unemployed Lutheran parishioners in Clairton, Pennsylvania, but for all the unemployed steel workers of the Pittsburgh area. He paid for his nonviolent resistance against the "financial interests controlling the steel plants" by being not only ordered out of his parish but formally defrocked by the Lutheran bishops in March 1985.

Another churchman, Desmond Tutu, the Anglican archbishop of South Africa and a Nobel Peace Prize laureate for his nonviolent antiapartheid stance, has become a world leader today. The South African blacks themselves have shown their strategy of nonviolence not only in boycotts but in the peaceful crowds at the funerals of other blacks who have been slaughtered by the police and military of the apartheid government.

Nonviolent resistance and civil disobedience know no boundaries of time or space. Nineteenth-century Protestant black churches of the American South, the sole organizations permitted the slaves, left a legacy to the civil rights movement of America. The pastors King, Senior and Junior, and black churches, became the basis for the

Southern Christian Leadership Conference. They provided the spirit and fire for the civil rights movement. The black churches also indirectly inspired the twentieth-century Catholic base communities of Central and South America, Africa and the Philippines.

Today it is through these base communities as well as the barrios of Latin America that liberation theology is energizing leadership in Third World nations circling the globe. North Americans are beginning to learn about liberation theology; some are even familiar with the names and works of Gustavo Gutierrez, Leonardo Boff, and Jon Sobrino. Far from stopping at the shores of South America, liberation theology has crossed the Caribbean to Haiti, where the church and its radio station played a part in the overthrow of the decades of the Duvaliers' dictatorship. Liberation theology had earlier crossed the Pacific to *conscientisize* clergy and laity in the first Catholic revolution in the modern world. And it took place without violence in the Philippines.

No matter who seeks to overthrow the government of Corazon Aquino in the coming years, the fact has been demonstrated once and for all that religious nonviolent resistance can and did topple the kingdom of greed perpetuated by Marcos. An actual witness to the revolution, the Reverend John Ryan, S. J., said in an interview in the Jesuit weekly, *America*:

"Had this revolutionary action not taken place . . . there's a real chance that within five years the Philippines would have become like El Salvador, where you would have had only a far left and a very far right. Right now, what you have is a reasonably centrist Government and a Government that has the real possibility not only of improving the lot of the Filipino people, but of getting rid of the excess of both the far left and the far right." [10]

Father Joseph P. Parkes, S. J., who arrived with Father Ryan in the Philippines three days before the revolution, told the interviewer, Father Thomas H. Stahel, S. J., associate editor of *America*, when he was asked what role priests and other religious persons had played among the leaders of the revolution:

"Mrs. Aquino . . . has made use in some cases of people who are priests but who are also very professionally competent. . . . It is important . . . to note the role that several people in the church played in actively promoting seminars on nonviolence. The principles of nonviolence were carefully inculcated in student leaders . . . the student leaders themselves played a tremendously effective role in getting people out on the streets with clear goals in mind as to what they wanted to bring about."[11]

Father Ryan said: ". . . the people—thousands upon thousands of civilians, many of them relatives of soldiers who were on Marcos's side—when they saw the army there, were pleading with them, begging them not to fire, saying to them, 'Don't get involved in acts of violence and killing.' All that had a tremendous effect on those soldiers. You actually saw people converting troops."

Father Parkes added: "That active nonviolence was a religious response to the situation in the Philippines was clear. Many people fasted for a couple of weeks after the election to help bring about peace. There was a tremendous devotion, particularly to Our Lady. . . . There is no question that the connection between active nonviolence and religious belief was very strong and played a powerful role among the college students, among the ordinary people, among the business and intellectual leaders who all gathered together to bring the Marcos government down. People really saw what they were doing as a religious response to a situation that had become utterly intolerable, a situation of grave injustice, a situation that, if allowed to continue, was going to bring about more chaos and more harm."[12]

We in the United States have seen, thanks to television, that "people power" trained in the gospel of Jesus' nonviolence can overthrow a dictator without bloodshed. President Aquino calls her government a provisional government rather than a revolutionary one. But revolutionary, it is. Father Ryan said: "I think a problem for Americans is that the word 'revolutionary' in recent years has been co-opted by the far left and by the Communist movement so that we perceive a 'revolutionary government' as something to be viewed with great suspicion. In point of fact, we are the children of the American Revolution, so the word 'revolution' isn't in itself a bad word."[13]

Like other great nonviolent revolutions, the boycotts of Gandhi and Martin Luther King, Jr. played a part in the revolution in the Philippines. Father Parkes said: "Once we got there the effectiveness of the boycott called by Corazon Aquino was very striking. Because it was selectively targeted, it became clear that this boycott was very well organized and was having dramatic effects on the economy of the country."[14]

Fasting and boycotting are traditional methods of nonviolent resistance. But both require discipline that generally comes from training either by religious or revolutionary groups. Today, though we lack revolutionary training we still have fasts, some of us during Lent, or before and during *Cursillos,* or as an offering to God.

It is the religious, trained in ascetical-mystical traditions, who could be effective as leaders in the hoped-for One Day Buyers' Boycott. Groups such as Pax Christi and others in which the vow of nonviolence is taken also have the background, and some even the training to persevere in nonviolence. It is doubtful whether the women and men who demonstrated at Selma could have maintained their nonviolent stance in the face of the violence used by the police had they not been steeped in the gospel of peace and surrender, as well as in specific strategic indoctrination. We all need training.

Gandhi said: "It is because we have at the present moment everybody claiming the right of conscience without going through any discipline whatsoever that there is so much untruth being delivered to a bewildered world."[15] A biographer of Gandhi, Eknath Easwaran, shares on his own discipline—two half-hour periods of meditation daily. Dom John Main says, "Meditation is above all a discipline." He also says that once you have learned to maintain this discipline on a twice daily basis, done for its sake alone, you can apply this discipline to the rest of your life. This enables you, I would add, to overcome being divided, ruled, bewildered, and confused by the warring words on the tube or in print. Then you will better be able to maintain your fasting and boycotting to get and keep us free of war and poverty—and from ourselves!

Remember, today it is a question of nonviolence or nonexistence. Our teacher and our Lord began his ministry in the discipline of prayer and fasting as a model for all of us. At the end he surrendered his life not to the Roman soldiers but to God. Even at the time of his arrest in the Garden, the nonviolent Jesus restored the ear of a soldier cut off by the impetuous Peter.

We need prayer and constant purification (fasting from one's defects as well as from food and things) if people power is to surrender to the practice of nonviolence. A surrendered nonviolent person is the only truly liberated person. I am reminded of a priest who had just returned from his Latin American mission to the poor. He said in a workshop at Notre Dame, "Only the just man can bring about the just society. The angry man either dies of frustration or sells out." I would add that only the surrendered person can bring about the just and peaceful society. *We* do the work through boycotts and other cultural actions, but leave the results to God (Acts 1:7–8).

Evelyn Underhill says that the social aspect of surrender is "a single unselfish yielding to those good social impulses which we all feel from time to time, and might take more seriously if we realized them as the impulsions of holy and creative Spirit pressing us toward novelty, giving us our chance; our small actualization of the universal tendency to the Divine . . . the obligation of response to those stirrings is laid on all who feel them; and unless some will first make this venture of faith, our possible future will never be achieved." [16]

We must learn to surrender to these "good social impulses" of which she spoke. Practicing what she preached, she did just that. At the most inauspicious time in England's history, when the Nazis were dropping bombs, killing her compatriots, she laid her reputation on the line by risking all for the ultimate gospel of Christ—the gospel of nonviolence. She became an outspoken and active pacifist during World War II, declaring, "On the question of war between man and man, she [the Church] cannot compromise." [17]

Her great contemporary in the Anglican Church, author Charles Williams, who edited her letters wrote: "Pacifism in her was the last development of the way she had followed; it was, in her and for her, our Lord's chosen method." [18]

Having done all, Evelyn Underhill stood on this principle of social surrender and wrote about it as the last stage of her liberation gospel, which she outlined while addressing Oxford students twenty years earlier. Then, she had prophetically deplored the kingdom of greed, the profit system, which was far more visible in its effects, then as now, than the kingdom of God. She asked her audience whether corporate repentance wasn't "the inevitable preliminary of social and spiritual advance."

Part of Underhill's definition of a saint describes what we have been saying of a sidewalk contemplative—one who seeks to "oppose in one way or another, by suffering, prayer, and work upon heroic levels of love and self-oblation, the mysterious downward drag within the world which we call sin. . . ."[19]

Father Rick Thomas, S. J., is founder and director of the Lord's Food Bank, which each week feeds more than 1,000 families who exist on the garbage dumps and in the barrios of Juarez, Mexico. He says, "We must pray and act to deliver the systems from their bondage to evil, the political, economical, social and religious systems that hold us in bondage today."[20]

It is the sin of systems that we must deliver from bondage to evil, not just the sin of persons, as Father Rick says. We have to do more than *feed* the hungry and *pray* for the destitute. We must *transform* the structures—those structures that put profit, power, and property before people. This may require a willingness to surrender our own economic well-being, whether we are working as a meat packer at a meat processing plant in the long Hormel strike of 1985–1986, or in a cherished vocation, as did the Reverend D. Douglas Roth, who was actually defrocked.

Social surrender involves the risk of blacklisting, as many writers, actors, singers, and musicians have found; jail sentences, as an increasing number are finding; and/or the ultimate risk of assassination. It involves keeping green the vision of the new society. It also requires being open to the new at all times, such as the revival of the workers' cooperative movement in the United States; changes in the status of women, of blacks, of ethnics, and of the aged. It may even require surrendering the "sanctity" of capitalism as the sole legitimate means of ownership of the means of production. And it might mean a closer look at the economy and government of the Scandinavian countries, or even the actual practice of socialism in a Third World country at peace, not at war, Tanzania. Until recently it was headed by an ardent Christian, who is also a Socialist, Julius Nyerere, whose nun constitutents I met when I was in Tanzania and Kenya in 1977.

A thirty-five-year-old client recently told me that he yearned to lead a life that is based on giving rather than taking, on cooperation rather than bloodthirsty competition. Though he didn't know it, he was talking about gospel justice. Happily for him, he was at least motivated enough to change: first to stop drinking, then when he was mentally as well as physically sober, to reorder his priorities in life. He chose the counterculture ambience that is emanated and absorbed by some members of Alcoholics Anonymous. The personal surrender in step 3 of AA's statement sooner or later may become a kind of social surrender based on the group's motto of "unity, service, recovery." Some members of AA even take cuts in their income in order to lead lives of service, a kind of love-in-action of which it was once said by Tertullian (d. 240): "See how these Christians love one another."[21]

As sidewalk contemplatives, we are committed to helping to establish the kingdom of God here on earth. In choosing to be redeemed by Jesus, we have chosen to help him redeem "the wretched of the earth" not only from the four horsemen of the Apocalypse but from the fifth horseman added in our century—nuclear holocaust.

Tools to Help Society Surrender
to the Reign of God

1. Meditate at least twice a day for a period of twenty-five minutes to free yourself from the finite and immerse yourself in the infinite. In other words, practice freedom from self—the true surrender.

2. Yield to the slightest impulse to help some person or group.
3. Practice turning the other cheek in your personal life. Apologize!
4. Reread the Sermon on the Mount and see what it says about surrender and nonviolence.
5. Practice step six of Breakthrough:
   "We surrendered to the reign of God in our lives—personally and socially—practicing obedience to God moment by moment."
6. Practice, one day at a time, putting people before things, peace before war, protection before exploitation.
7. Put your prayer where your action is./Put your action where your prayer is.

   This means that in any social situation, prayer group, or community action, you should surrender to the good social impulse that comes from the Spirit, not to your old, unredeemed self.
8. *Fiat voluntas tua*—"Thy will be done" (Matt. 6:10).

EIGHT

Breakthrough Step Seven:
UNION

Step Seven: To get in and stay in union with God and his kingdom, we practiced these steps personally and in the world around us.

In 1979 I overdosed, not on booze, the drug of my choice as a young woman, but on publicity before and after the Susan B. Anthony dollar was issued by Rosalynn Carter at the White House. Because of Aunt Susan's fame and our name, I have been covered by the press on numerous occasions since I was four years old. But publicity peaked at an all-time high on June 20, 1979, the day Mrs. Carter invited my family and me to the ceremony. It was being held nine days in advance of the issuing of the Anthony dollar by the Federal Reserve because the president and Mrs. Carter were due in Japan on June 29.

My sister Charlotte and I were to share the platform with Mrs. Carter, Mrs. Walter Mondale, wife of the then vice-president, and then secretary of the treasury, W. Michael Blumenthal. The other guests sat on straight-backed chairs on the sunny lawn of the South Portico. I had not been the guest of a first lady since 1943, when Mrs. Roosevelt had me take tea with her à deux on the publication of my first book, *Out of the Kitchen—Into the War.* Charlotte and I were invited to pose for photos alone with Mrs. Carter and a huge mock-up of the unflattering portrait of Aunt Susan that had alas been engraved on the dollar by the U.S. Treasury. The photo of the three of us, plus Aunt Susan's image, I would learn later from calls and letters, was wired around the world.

Our afternoon at the White House took place after a rushed lecture in Beverly Hills that had delayed my arrival in Washington until late the previous night. Nor was there to be any letup in the next nine days—with lectures, press interviews and appearances, climaxed by the Federal Reserve Bank's official ceremony on June 29, when the bank and I formally sent forth the Anthony dollar into general circulation.

A few days later I awoke in my apartment in Deerfield Beach feeling fragmented, atomized, separated from my center. I was edgy, almost jittery, like my old alcoholic self before I sobered up. But I was now thirty-three years sober. It was July 4, 1979. But I certainly didn't feel like celebrating any more historical events after my overexposure to and for Anthony history in the past months. I decided to take the day off. I left my phone off the hook. I propped myself up on my pillows, picked up my Bible and clipboard, and began praying.

Suddenly I found myself scrawling: "All I really want, Lord, is to be 'hid with Christ in God.'" Where did that come from? I knew it was St. Paul's, but which letter? I went to the bookcase and pulled out my Concordance. It was Col. 3:3. I turned to it and read in my Bible: "For you have died, and your life is hid with Christ in God." I climbed back into bed with my clipboard and pen. To me " . . . hid with Christ in God" meant union with God. I turned to John 17, the priestly prayer of Jesus. He had prayed for all of us believers, not just Apostles who were with him at the Last Supper:

> I . . . pray . . . also for those who will believe in me through their [the apostles'] word, that all may be one as you, Father, are in me, and I in you; I pray that they may be (one) in us, that the world may believe that you sent me. I have given them the glory you gave me that they may be one, as we are one—I living in them, you living in me—that their unity may be complete (John 17:20–23).

Except for my inviolate prayer time in the early morning, and some peaceful hours on planes while flying from one lecture to another how stingy was the time I had spent in recent months "hid with Christ in God." How rarely I had meditated on Jesus' words that he lived in me, had begun to live in me even before I knew him, when those words came to me back in 1960: "If I had spent as much time on God in the past twenty-five years as I have spent on men, I would be a saint."

Now, in 1979, I wrote on my clipboard, "It is not men who have distracted and diverted me during the past year. It is the celebrity, the hype, reflecting on my inherited name and Aunt Susan's—not my fame. True, I am a small-time queen of the road. But, also true, I have often acted like a two-bit prima donna, becoming overinflated on the publicity her name brought me." I pondered some more. Had I been acting on some kind of backlash from the total obscurity that had been forced upon me during my nine months at the convent? The novice mistress had forbidden any kind of ministry on my part, even helping alcoholics; she forbade my reading any theology. Nor could I speak out in prayer groups, and certainly I could never mention that I had written books. During those nine months I had been erased as a fifty-nine-year-old achiever of some accomplishment.

The involuntary humility had cut deeper than I had realized. In fact, it had taken an extraordinary press and television blitz to readers and viewers to restore my false ego. That fluke came only three months after the novice mistress bounced me in June 1976. A U.S. Senate press gallery and radio conference, and a reception of the Senate Subcommittee on Alcoholism honoring my thirty years of sobriety and work for alcoholics had catapulted me onto a national television quiz show not once but five weeks running. I answered questions on women's rights, trying to win the $124,000 prize to relieve my postconvent pauperism. Though I won only $16,000 in money, as my friend Marty Mann said, I had won a "new career as national and international lecturer at the age of sixty." I basked in the spotlight whether I was lecturing on alcoholism, feminism, or mysticism, or giving retreats to alcoholic women and men.

I was especially lionized when I was flown from Florida to San Diego as one of the celebrity alcoholics coming out of the closet as such, and made a keynote speaker for the Congress of Task Forces on Women and Alcoholism. Though night had fallen when I arrived in San Diego after the long flight, I was impelled to put on my walking shoes and leave the palatial Louis Quinze room with its crystal chandeliers that the council had booked for me. I walked up darkened C Street on a pilgrimage. Few of us get the chance to return to the scene of our meeting with our true love. Now I searched for the place where I had first met Jesus. The walk seemed long and scary in the dimly-lit street. In fact, the only sign of life and light was the YMCA, where I stopped to find out whether the YWCA building I sought had been torn down. The black clerk looked at me appraisingly and said, "It's up two blocks, but you don't want a room there, do you? They don't rent rooms anymore."

I assured him that I didn't want a room and went to the YWCA. It was blaring with rock music doubly amplified, and the joyful shouts of young Mexicans and Anglos having their Friday night bash. Bewildered and disappointed, I spoke to the only adult present, a Mexican woman. "This is where I stayed seventeen years ago, upstairs in Room 404," I said. "I'd like to see the room." She said I should come back on Monday.

It was not until after the press conference, the banquet, and my speech to the women that I could put on my walking shoes again. I walked the seven blocks from the Westgate Hotel to the five-story, red-tile-roofed YWCA. A Mrs. Rose Randall, secretary, led me up the four flights of dusty stairs of the now-abandoned residential floors. She took me to Room 404, saying, "Having heard your story, I know you want to be alone."

I could hardly believe I was here again in this little room with the tan bureau and the tan metal bed and beige walls. Even shabbier than when I had last seen it, it now looked dim and forlorn. Then a shaft of sunlight lit it up and drew me to the window. I looked out, as I had done so long ago, at the blue bay of San Diego and beyond to the red turrets of the massive white majesty of the Hotel del Coronada. Here in this bare, brown, abandoned room, I had met my last love—the longest, the best—on October 7, 1960. Here it was that Jesus had appeared to my mind's eye and said, "I am God, not just man. Before Abraham was, I am."

I prayed and thanked him for taking over my life on that day, unfaithful lover though I have been. I vowed to reconsecrate myself to him, to set aside the time that is left for Jesus. And though I had never scrawled graffiti on subways, I took out my pen and wrote on the soon-to-be-painted wall:

Susan Anthony met Jesus here, October 7, 1960
Returned November 1971
Returned May 3, 1977. Alleluia! Revelations 2:4–5

Back at the Westgate I pondered the Revelations verses: "But I have this against you, that you have abandoned the love you had at first. Remember then from what you have fallen, repent and do the works you did at first. If not, I will come to you and remove your lampstand from its place, unless you repent" (2:4–5).

I sat and sought discernment. Had I indeed abandoned the love I had at first, the works I did at first? Had I let my ardor grow dim, forgotten my "goal for the prize of the upward call of God in Christ Jesus" (Phil. 3:14)—the goal of union with God? After I met Jesus he led me step by step toward my goal—my reception in the church, my theological studies and teaching, my private vows, even my unsuccessful attempt to live as a sister in community. Now on July 4, 1979 I was being prodded by the Lord to give priority once more to the goal of union with him, to write it once again more on the frontlets of my head. I must be "hid with Christ in God" and/or even to be able to say one day, "I have been crucified with Christ; it is no longer I who live, but Christ who lives in me . . . "(Gal. 2:20).

The good news is that no matter how often I have failed, I have been repeatedly brought back to the goal—the goal of seeking the same self-oblivion in God that I once found in booze. The good news is that the Christed self has "chosen the good portion, which shall not be taken away from her" (Luke 10:42). Nor *can* it be taken away. Once we have been granted a tasting knowledge of

God, it cannot be taken away from us permanently unless we reject it permanently. We can neglect it as I often have, bury it under the tyranny of trivia, even commit sins against charity. But it will be restored to us when we arise and go to our Father.

It would be wonderful to have a continuous, unbroken state of conscious union with God as some of the great mystics have. But even intermittent, interrupted union with God is beter than no union at all. Dr. Robert Lifton, the Yale psychohistorian, uses the phrase "experiential transcendence" in his works to describe "a psychic state—one so intense and all encompassing that time and death disappear. This state is the classical mode of the mystic."[1]

Dorothee Soelle, the German theologian, says mysticism "is a perception of God through experience . . . gained not through books, not through the authority of religious teachings, not through the so-called priestly office, but through the life experiences of human beings, experiences that are articulated and reflected upon in religious language but that first come to people in what they encounter in life, independent of the church's institutions."[2] I would add, as does Evelyn Underhill, that the overwhelming majority of mystics, at least those who are recorded anywhere, are those who have in some way become acquainted with the experiences or teachings of their mystic predecessors.

I have also found that the stages of mystical growth can be taught to people of all ages, faith, race, or sex. As long as you don't call the journey "mystical," you can convey the message of mysticism to anyone. Following my conversion to Jesus as Lord, I started the first Breakthrough group, calling it Mismated Anonymous. I used the seven steps of Breakthrough to the New Self, drawn from the twelve steps of AA and the classic mystic way. The stages were not only acceptable to this heterogeneous group of "mismateds" but intelligible. That season I daily shared the steps with a mixture of health-food buffs and local residents of Nogales, Arizona, at the Royal Road health resort. Later, while doing my doctoral in theology my classmates and I gathered in a Breakthrough group, praying and sharing at Saint Mary's Graduate School of Theology in Indiana.

I taught my first academic class in the steps of Breakthrough to high-school seniors at Saint Mary's Academy in South Bend. The course I gave them for one semester is printed in my doctoral dissertation, *The Prayer Supported Apostle.* That summer I taught the mystic way—calling it Breakthrough to priests, nuns, and graduate students at Saint Mary's College Graduate School of Theology before and after the weekend conference that launched Breakthrough as the first spontaneous prayer group conference in the church in 1965.

When I began teaching Scripture and theology at Marymount College, Boca Raton, in the fall of 1965, I started Breakthrough classes and small groups in Florida. The first to come were the freshmen and sophomore students who met weekly at my cottage near the beach, Casa de la Paloma, for four years. We walked the beach meditating in silence under the stars, returned home, sat on the floor with soft drinks, and shared any "glimpses" of God, or any other aspect of our inner life. We shared biblical and other readings they had selected from a list I made for them. We put on a large prayer conference at Marymount, with adults and students attending. The religious writer, the late Catherine Marshall spoke for us. Our student Breakthrough group formed the core group working on the national prayer vigil to win my freedom from the deportation order in 1969.

Today when my whereabouts are publicized through news or television coverage, I hear from those Breakthrough students. They write or call to tell me that they have never forgotten the steps of Breakthrough. Some even bought *Survival Kit* when it was published and republished, because it reminds them of how to get in union with God and stay in union.

In addition to the student group at Marymount, a group of adult women began studying and practicing Breakthrough with me in another class. Later when we moved off campus to a church, we came right out and called it studying mysticism, using not only Scripture but Evelyn Underhill's classic, *Mysticism,* on the seven stages of the mystical life. That class lasted six years, from 1968 to

1974. During those years some of us had also founded Socially Concerned Contemplative to bring the steps of Breakthrough into action for the new society as well as the new self. The hot center of my attention had now moved to a synthesis of the prayerful transformation of society as well as the self. We sought to emulate the mystics in our Judeo-Christian tradition. They can never rest in silence and solitude on their Mount Carmel or Mount Athos. Some of them must get back down to the marketplace as Teresa of Avila did—become a sidewalk contemplative, taking to the streets as the French author Charles Peguy said, and Dorothy Day did, and to where the poor are, as she, Mother Theresa, and others have done throughout the centuries.

Since Vatican II, missionaries and priests have swelled the number of sidewalk contemplatives who have paid the ultimate price, especially in South and Central America for their work for the poor. Survivors tell their own stories of torture and the martyrdom of others. Biographers write of the archbishop of El Salvador, Oscar Romero, who was assassinated at the altar in his cathedral. Others have been portrayed in film documentaries or television stories, including the three nuns and Jean Donovan, the church worker, who were murdered in 1980 by El Salvador security forces.

Still others have been the subject of fiction, such as Sister Justin in Robert Stone's great novel *A Flag for Sunrise*. Sister Justin not only served as a nurse but became active as a partisan with the peasants against the dictatorship in the anonymous Central American country. She incurred the wrath not only of the *National Guardia* of the dictatorship but of the U.S. security forces. Finally she is arrested and forced by Officer Campos to ride in the jeep with him to the *Justicia*. There she sees the corpses of her peasant friends "stacked in piles, swelling in the sun, stinking and beset with flies...."

Lieutenant Campos begins the torture of Sister Justin with a beating so severe that "she was awash in all the shameful juices of living." Next he applies electricity that shook loose her bones so badly that "she could only live between shocks." She knows that she is dying. But even as the shocks go through her, a current "greater than electricity" dominates her and she knows something more than the torture of dying. She knows she is not alone, that Christ is with her. At the last she says to her killer, "Behold the handmaid of the Lord." [3]

When I was a college student at the University of Rochester, my heroine in fiction was Mary French, a dropout from a leading women's college in the novel *The Big Money* by John Dos Passos. He had drawn what I thought then, and continue to think today, was a true portrait of a middle-class, intellectual radical of her era. Though I became a college radical twenty years later than she, I could still identify with Mary's desire to change the system, to free the oppressed, to keep the world out of World War II. As with Mary, God played no part in my life. Unlike Mary, my commitment to the left was so diluted by booze that it claimed more and more of my devotion and took me to men and places that were definitely not working-class. That was all the more reason for me to admire Mary French, since I could not emulate her revolutionary heroism.

Along comes Sister Justin, one of *today's* heroines, who shares Mary French's commitment to the poor but is also rooted in a commitment to Jesus. Sister Justin synthesizes what we have been talking about in this book—a sidewalk contemplative-in-process.

In his book *The Wounded Healer* Henri Nouwen says we do not have to divide ourselves into religious or mystical versus revolutionary; or the mystical *way* versus the revolutionary way: The two ways, says Nouwen, are not opposites; they are "two sides of the same human mode of experiential transcendence." [4] Mysticism is the inner way; revolutionary struggle is the outer way.

Nouwen says that the revolutionary "becomes aware that the choice is no longer between his world and a better world, but between no world and a new world. It is the way of the man [or woman] who says: Revolution is better than suicide. This man is deeply convinced that our world is heading for the edge of the cliff. . . ." [5] The revolutionary, he says, is seeking not a better self but a new self. He or she is willing to give life itself for the new self and the new society, and is committed to the view "that it is better to give your life than to take it. . . ." Nouwen continues: "It is certainly not surprising that the great revolutionary leaders and the great contemplatives of our time meet in their common concern to liberate nuclear man from his paralysis."[6]

Here some twentieth-century sidewalk contemplatives come to mind, such as Thomas Merton, Ernesto Cardenales and Daniel Berrigan. But for most Christians, Jesus remains the model of the union of revolution and mysticism in one person, the sign that they cannot be separated in the human being's search for experiential transcendence. Changing the self and changing society are not separate tasks," says Nouwen but "are as interconnected as the two beams of the cross."[7]

To help unite these often separated beams of the cross has been the major challenge of my life as a Christian. And I have tried to meet this challenge in a language and praxis acceptable for today. Most people, especially the young, are turned off by, or completely unaware of what is the mystical way, let alone the language used to describe it in the spiritual classics. Dorothee Soelle says, " . . . the result of that is . . . that these experiences go uncommunicated to others, are lost and forgotten. We are unable to tell anyone else the most important experiences we have."[8]

Yet, says R. C. Zaehner: "There still remains a minority [of young people, SBA], sometimes a very vocal one, which feels that life must ultimately lack meaning unless it has a transcendental dimension . . . unless it is in some way anchored in eternity. More often than one thinks, perhaps, young people do have such 'intimations of immortality' which, though they may be vague enough, nevertheless make them think that behind the physical world there lies another world which is more real than the world of space and time simply because they sense, again however vaguely, that this other world can and does make itself felt on rare occasions, usually in moments of solitude and in natural surroundings of exceptional beauty—mountains, the sea, the blossoming of spring, and of course, sunsets. . . . Of the 400 young people to whom the questionnaire [on such revelations] was sent 222 returned positive answers."[9]

Walker Percy, one of the outstanding Christian novelists of our time and nation, writes: "In a post-religious age, the only transcendence open to the self is self-transcendence, that is, the transcending of the world by the self. The available modes of transcendence in such an age are science and art." [10]

Soelle found only one student out of a class she taught at Union Theological Seminary who dared even raise her hand and answer the professor's question on religious experience. A week later the student reported on two examples of experiential transcendence that were beyond self-transcendence in art or science. Her first experience took place when she was fourteen. She had been reading before going to sleep, and awoke at four in the morning, stimulated by what she had been reading. She walked out into the winter night, gazing up at the stars. Then she had, says Soelle, "a feeling of happiness that was unique for her, a feeling of unity with all of life, with God, an experience of overpowering clarity and joy, a sense of being cared for and borne up.... I am indestructible; I am one with the All."

The student said this religious experience did not repeat itself until years later when she took part in a big demonstration against the Vietnam War. Soelle reports: "There, too, she felt cared for, a part of the All, felt herself together with others participating in the truth of the All. For her, both these experiences belonged together under the heading 'religious experience.'" [11]

I would add that the student was sharing both a soli*tary* religious experience and a soli*dary* one. As an adolescent she felt soli*tary* union with the All. Nine years later she felt in addition soli*dary* union with her sisters and brothers, transcending the dangers and difficulties of the demonstration through a sense of union with them. Again, I think we must be both soli*tary* and soli*dary* as sidewalk contemplatives. As Nouwen has said, these modes are as "interconnected as the two beams of the cross."

We differ from the unbeliever with whom we unite in the movements for peace and justice in that we cannot limit ourselves to the natural. We are rooted and grounded in trying to become, as Underhill says, a person whose "whole life, personal, social, intellectual and mystical is lived in supernatural regard." [12] As Christians, many of us try to live in supernatural regard at least some of the time. We try to find God in our personal dark nights under the threat of the impersonal nuclear extinction that daily comes closer.

The sidewalk contemplative as distinct from the secular activist seeks to be a "chosen vessel of the redeeming, transforming, creative love of God." [13] Because of this the sidewalk contemplative is less likely than the secular activist to become depressed at the state of the world, or demagogic at the sound and the fury of his or her own actions.

I have been blessed since college days to meet and work with such "chosen vessels"—Lyal Maie Reynolds Shoemaker of North Carolina was one of the first. It was with great joy, therefore, that fifty years later I learned firsthand that North Carolina is still in the vanguard of spiritualizing and socializing movements. Through the Benedictine Christian Meditation Center at Montreal, I heard of an innovative spirituality "in the heart of the Bible belt." I telephoned to find out more from Dr. Richard Hoffman, the assistant to the president of Mars Hill College and learned that he is starting a center that unites the traditions of contemplative prayer with the great social issues of our time, especially peace. Dr. Hoffman has been a meditator in the Dom John Main tradition for more than two years. Part of his 1985–1986 sabbatical was spent journeying to India to pray and meditate with Hindus and Buddhists.

Mars Hill College pioneered in 1962 as the first private white college in North Carolina to accept black students and Indians of all tribes. It provides facilities for Catholics to worship on campus, and holds ecumenical conferences. Liberation theologians and East-West leaders meet on this small southern campus to worship and reflect. When I interviewed Dr. Hoffman last spring he said he will be bringing to campus other leaders to share insights on contemplation and social issues. Mars Hill undergraduates may even join the growing number of solitaries and solidaries in bridge movements throughout Latin America and Africa as well as in the United States. And in the summer of 1986 Mars Hill offered Elderhostel students courses entitled "The Church and Social Change in Central and South America," taught by Dr. Hoffman; "The Contemplative Life and Social Action: Monastic Experience" and "Toward a Postmodern Theology: The Christian and Jewish Experiences in America," taught by others.

I don't know why I should be surprised (but I was) that liberation theology, which has reached the outermost edges of the world, has reached a North American Bible belt college. After all, liberation theology *is* Christian, despite the implications of some of its critics. Liberation theology combines prayer and praxis for the goal of the "transformation and building of society." Only spiritual power can overcome "spiritual wickedness in high places" (Eph. 6:12). But prayer is quickened by practice, as Jesus showed descending from solitary prayer on the mountaintop to soli*d*ary action in the marketplace—teaching, healing, rescuing the people. From there he leaped *solitary* to the cross in his once-for-all act of holy redemption.

Liberation theology is part of today's manifestation of humanity's spiritual goal of union with God and union with each other. It even goes a step further, declaring that there is union of salvation and secular history. This vision is put forth by the father of liberation theology, Gustavo Gutierrez, in the following statement:

> History is one . . . there are not two histories, one profane and one sacred. . . . Rather there is only one human destiny, irreversibly assumed by Christ, the Lord of history. His redemptive work embraces all the dimensions of existence and brings them to their fullness. The history of salvation is the very heart of human history. . . . The historical destiny of humanity must be placed definitively in the salvific horizon . . . there is only one history—a Christo-finalized history.[14]

Dorothee Soelle links mysticism, feminism, and liberation. She says their common denominator is that "there are people who are involved in the search for non-authoritarian human relationships and who are working toward the abolition of class rule and class injustice." She does not think liberation takes place when there is merely

"a change in government and another clique comes to power...." [15]
She tells a story of true liberation in the sense she means. A journalist in Nicaragua asked a seventy-two-year-old woman who was standing in front of a school that the Sandinistas had built in a rural prov-
ince, "Can you read?" The old woman answered, "Not yet."

Soelle says this shows that a major dimension of liberation is "an
economy which is not geared to the increase of profits alone." It
certainly would not raise the gross national product a bit to teach a
seventy-two-year-old woman to read. "She felt a new hope," Soelle
says. "Her psychological state had been altered by the revolution." [16]

And I would add that the promise of the gospel was being carried
out. Liberating this old woman from illiteracy shows there is a
priority on trying to bring an abundant life to her "on earth, as it is
in heaven."

A giant leap forward has been the growing unity among churches
in our century—and not only between Catholic and Protestant.
John Paul II became the first pope in history to meet with a Jewish
rabbi (of Rome's leading synagogue) on the second Sunday of Easter
1986. We have also seen a growing unity in the mysticism of the
East and the West, publicized by the trek of youth, some of them
rock stars, to the East in the 1960s and the 1970s. They brought
home what they had learned in Eastern meditation. A more lasting
impact has been that of the retrieval by Dom John Main and others
in the twentieth century of the Christian basis of meditation introduced in the fifth century.

Less known but of long standing has been the unity of the Eastern
Orthodox churches, especially the Russian Orthodox with some of
our own Protestant churches. I learned about this in 1984 while
participating in one of the largest-ever peace pilgrimages to the Soviet Union sponsored by the National Council of Churches of Christ
in America. I had met my first Russian Orthodox archbishop a few
miles from home at a Methodist church in Delray Beach, Florida. It
was my great joy to interview Archbishop Makary while I was in
Kiev in 1982, and attend his Mass. The luminosity of the Russian
Orthodox service in the beautiful, unique churches moved me aes-

thetically as well as spiritually. In1984, thanks to the Russian Orthodox invitation, we seldom passed a day without attending church in the Soviet Union. Equally impressive was the ardor and youth of the congregations, and the crowds. There are 40 million Russian Orthodox in the Soviet Union today. We Catholics were outnumbered (only 18 out of the 266 pilgrims) in 1984. Protestant social justice roots in the United States go back as far as the eithteenth century. In our century powerful voices, such as Reinhold Niebuhr and Walter Rauschenbusch, have led the way for us Catholics to follow in the wake of Vatican II.

My dream is that this unity with each other, built upon each one's growth toward union with God, will lead to the cultural action I have urged throughout this book—the One Day Buyers' Boycott. Meditation and prayer groups will have to work closely with an increasing number of peace and justice groups, both in and out of the churches. If it is to succeed spiritually and socially, however, the boycott must be built upon the solid foundation of prayer—prayer in the months of preparation needed for the boycott; prayer on the boycott picket lines; and prayer in our own churches and those of others before and afterward.

I have been given a foretaste of union in diversity by two recent films. One was the ending of the film *Places in the Heart*. Taking communion together in a Texas Protestant church were murdered and murderer, black and white, sexual rivals, and business competitors. Of course, to me it was a taste of heaven. The other film was *The Color Purple*. The bar flies, drawn by the gospel music pouring out of the church, leave the bar, prance, singing a mixture of blues and gospel, with horns blaring, and march like the saints to embrace the church congregation and choir with shouts of glory.

In real life I tasted union in November 1985. A few dozen of us stood with lighted candles singing and sharing with an interfaith panel of clergy and rabbis—praying for the success of the Summit between Reagan and Gorbachev. We had hoped to hold our vigil on the beach, but in the rainy night St. Gregory's Episcopal Church gave us sanctuary. And I was glad, because in the softly lighted church I could see the faces of my coworkers for peace shining not only with the union we felt with each other but with "something more" that filled the church, uniting us with the God of our understanding in the profound hope that he alone gives to a world in disarray. For me it was one of those rare moments of conscious union with God *and* union with my sisters and brothers. Perhaps, I had been given it because I had been obedient to his command to us to come out on a dark and stormy night to share our hope.

Tools for Getting in and Staying in Union with God and His Kingdom

1. Meditate daily on step seven.
2. Grade yourself on how well you are carrying the message while practicing the seven steps of Breakthrough one day at a time.
3. Meet at least once a month with others who seek to liberate the new self and usher in the new society.
4. Pray daily for the redemption of society as well as for personal redemption.
5. Meditate on: "The vision of God for all requires the kingdom of God for all / The kingdom of God for all requires the vision of God for all."
6. Meditate on the statement that the kingdom of God on earth requires "that we may be able to lead undisturbed and tranquil lives in perfect piety and dignity" (1 Tim. 2:2).
7. Meditate on your vision of "a society that renders contemplation possible for its members."

NINE.

TESTAMENT

The Spirit has put and kept me on the spiral way of Breakthrough, mounting from misplaced mystic to prayer-supported apostle to sidewalk contemplative-in-process. But the way for me has not ended there. I dare to seek the high road of the redemptive revolutionary in the steps of the Redeemer and those whom he has touched.

Jesus redeemed me not as a solitary person only but as a potential coredeemer who is solidary with the human race. I am not living the *whole* gospel unless I try to become like him and help to deliver humanity from its paralysis and oppression. Jesus was a revolutionary because he turned the world upside down. We need to turn our world upside down, trading our self-obsession for union with Christ's consciousness.

I have been inspired by three redemptive revolutions. Aunt Susan led the women's revolution, which is, of course, my heritage. But so is the black revolution, led in our century by Martin Luther King, Jr. and begun by my family and their friends in the nineteenth century. In our time we have witnessed Gandhi's liberation of India through a truly redemptive revolution. All three revolutions—of women, blacks, and India—have been nonviolent, carried out by prayer and fasting, boycotts, picket lines, civil disobedience, and lobbying.

Evelyn Underhill's description of a saint, I think, also defines a redemptive revolutionary when she writes that he or she is "To help,

save, and enlighten by his [her] loving actions and contemplations: . . ."
Those of you who have become sidewalk contemplatives, willing to
take the ultimate risk, are redemptive revolutionaries-in-process, because, like the saints, you "oppose in one way or another, by suffering, prayer and work upon heroic levels of love and self-oblation, the
mysterious downward drag within the world which we call sin."[1]

Most of us are so brainwashed by the mighty that we are afraid to
call ourselves revolutionaries of any kind. Yet every American is
born a revolutionary by virtue of the American Revolution, which
gave us our birth as a nation from a colony, and transformed us
from being subjects of the crown into citizens of the republic. Aunt
Susan and Elizabeth Cady Stanton called their newspaper *The Revolution* because they advocated a revolution in the status of women.
The English mystic-scholar and my spiritual mother, Evelyn Underhill, could be called a redemptive revolutionary. It was indeed a
redemptive and a revolutionary act for her to come out publicly as a
pacifist when her country was about to be invaded by the Nazis in
World War II.

A redemptive revolutionary, as distinct from a secular revolutionary, seeks a revolution that would establish a society that renders
contemplation possible for its members, not just a spiritual, financial,
racial, or family elite. We have been robbed by the war society that
would have us betray our revolutionary past, our redemptive grace,
and our posterity. It took me some time to recognize Aunt Susan's
work for woman suffrage as the longest nonviolent revolution in
our history; and that her fortitude, despite constant failure, was in
itself redemptive. But no one can ignore the fact that Gandhi's revolution, based on prayer, fasting and nonviolence, was redemptive;
nor that the black revolutions led by Martin Luther King, Jr. in the
1960s and by the victims of apartheid in South Africa today are
redemptive despite the violence perpetrated against them. I admire
all of these workers and sufferers for peace. I would not be satisfied
to be a secular revolutionary, much as I admire some of them, especially Rosa Luxemburg, who was martyred in Germany in 1919 for
the cause of peace and justice.

If, however, I a Christian were to seek secular revolution only, then Christ has died in vain. Jesus Christ makes the difference in my life. Without him there would have been no personal revolution overthrowing my old self and establishing the new self. Without him there can be no redemptive revolution overthrowing the old society and establishing the new society, the kingdom of God on earth. To bring about that revolution we need redemptive souls— committed, daring, dedicated.

We need to be prodigal in giving and spending our lives, and/or our silver in the coredemptive work our world so desperately needs to save it from social sin, sickness, and nuclear annihilation. I want to stand up and be counted in my time as a redemptive revolutionary, as were my ancestors in their revolutions for American independence, for abolition of slavery, and for abolition of women's oppression. It was inevitable that Aunt Susan and Elizabeth Cady Stanton chose for their newspaper, *The Revolution*, the motto:

> Men, their rights, and nothing more:
> Women, their rights, and nothing less.

Perhaps we could paraphrase that today:

> The mighty, their rights, and nothing more.
> The poor, their rights, and nothing less.

And I would add, as did Aunt Susan, the old revolutionary slogan:

> Resistance to tyranny is obedience to God!

that Mary the Mother of God expressed:

> . . . he has filled the hungry with good things, and the rich
> he has sent empty away (Luke 1:53).

NOTES

CHAPTER 1. CONVERT

1. Susan B. Anthony, *The Ghost in My Life* (New York: Chosen Books, 1971), pp. 214–15.
2. Susan B. Anthony, *The Prayer Supported Apostle* (Notre Dame, IN: Catholic Action, 1965).
3. The full prayer may be found in Walter M. Abbott, ed., *The Documents of Vatican II* (New York: Herder and Herder, 1966), p. 793.
4. Quoted in P. W. Martin, *Experiment in Depth: A Study of the Work of Jung, Eliot, and Toynbee* (New York: Pantheon Books, 1955), p. 252.
5. Aldous Huxley, *The Perennial Philosophy* (New York: Harper/Colophon Books, 1945), p. 294.
6. *The Prayer Supported Apostle*, pp. 61–66.
7. Susan B. Anthony, *Survival Kit* (1st ed., New York: New American Library, 1972; 2nd ed., Minneapolis: CompCare, 1981).

CHAPTER 2. BREAKTHROUGH STEP ONE: ADMISSION AND AWAKENING

1. Susan B. Anthony, "The Anatomy of a Conversion," unpublished master's thesis, Saint Mary's Graduate School of Theology, Notre Dame, Indiana, 1963.
2. Alcoholics Anonymous World Service, Inc., *"Pass It On:" The Story of Bill Wilson and How the A.A. Message Reached the World* (New York: Alcoholics Anonymous World Service, Inc., 1984), pp. 135 ff.

3. Ibid., p. 120.
4. Ibid., p. 121.
5. Ibid., p. 123.
6. William James, *The Varieties of Religious Experience: A Study in Human Nature* (1902; New York: Modern Library, 1929).
7. "*Pass It On,*" p. 124.
8. James, *The Varieties of Religious Experience*, p. 498.
9. Ibid., p. 499.
10. Ibid.
11. Alcoholics Anonymous Publishing, Inc., *Alcoholics Anonymous: The Story of How Many Thousands of Men and Women Have Recovered from Alcoholism*, new and rev. ed. (New York: Alcoholics Anonymous Publishing, Inc., 1955), pp. 59–60.
12. Dorothee Soelle, *The Arms Race Kills Even Without War*, trans. Gerhard Elston (Philadelphia: Fortress Press, 1983), p. 2.
13. Ibid., pp. 2–3.
14. Ibid., pp. 3–4.
15. Ibid., p. 4.
16. Emma Lazarus, "The New Colossus: Inscription for the Statue of Liberty, New York Harbor, 1886," in John Bartlett, *Familiar Quotations*, 12th ed., rev. and enl. (Boston: Little, Brown & Co., 1951) p. 694.
17. Ibid.
18. R. C. Zaehner, *Concordant Discord* (Oxford: Clarendon Press, 1970), p. 395.
19. Gustavo Gutierrez, *A Theology of Liberation*, trans. and ed. Sister Caridad Inda and John Eagleson (Maryknoll, NY: Orbis Books, 1973), p. 91. Paulo Freire, *Pedagogy of the Oppressed*, trans. Myra Bergman (New York: Seabury Press, 1970).
20. Soelle, *The Arms Race Kills*, p. 19.
21. Ibid.

CHAPTER 3. BREAKTHROUGH STEP TWO: PRAYER

1. Susan B. Anthony, *The Prayer Supported Apostle* (Notre Dame, IN: Catholic Action, 1965), p. 9.
2. Quoted in Maurice Nédoncelle, *God's Encounter with Man*, trans. A. Manson (New York: Sheed and Ward, 1964), p. viii.

3. Kenneth E. Kirk, *The Vision of God*, 2nd ed. (London: Longmans, Green and Co., 1931), p. 1.
4. Ibid., p. 431.
5. Henri Bremond, *Introduction à la Philosophie de la Prière* (Paris: Bloud et Gay, 1929), p. 96.
6. *Summa Theologica*, II–II, Q. 83, arts. 6 and 2 respectively, quoted from the First Complete American Edition in 3 vols. (New York: Benziger Brothers, 1947), p. 1538. St. Thomas elaborates on petition in arts. 1–17.
7. John Main, *Letters from the Heart: Christian Monasticism and the Renewal of Community* (New York: Crossroad, 1985).
8. Interview with Dom Laurence Freeman, Fort Myers Beach, Florida, 22 February 1986. See also his book, *Light Within: The Inner Path of Meditation* (New York: Crossroad, 1987).
9. Jacques and Raissa Maritain, *Prayer and Intelligence*, trans. Algar Thorold (London: Sheed and Ward, 1928), pp. 19–21.
10. First published in *The Prayer Supported Apostle*, p. 55.

CHAPTER 4. BREAKTHROUGH STEP THREE: CLEANSING

1. Evelyn Underhill, *The Spiritual Life* (London: Hodder and Stoughton, 1955), p. 53.
2. Henry Hill Collins, Jr., *America's Own Refugees* (Princeton, NJ: Princeton University Press, 1941).
3. *Miami Herald*, 21 November 1985.
4. Pope Paul VI, *Populorum Progressio* (Boston: Daughters of St. Paul, 1971), footnote 33.
5. *Justice in the World* (Boston: Daughters of St. Paul, 1971).
6. Ibid., p. 3.
7. Ibid., pp. 16–17.
8. Ibid., p. 16.
9. Ibid., pp. 15–16.
10. Frederick Herzon, *Justice Church: The New Function of the Church in North American Christianity* (Maryknoll, NY: Orbis Books, 1980), p. 82.
11. Ibid.
12. Ibid., p. 134.

13. Paulo Freire, *Pedagogy of the Oppressed*, trans. Myra Bergman Ramos (New York: Seabury Press, 1970), p. 176.
14. Thomas J. Reese, S.J., "Strike for Peace," *America*, 16 July 1983, p. 24.
15. *Miami Herald*, 23 March 1986.
16. Ibid.
17. Ibid.
18. William James, *The Varieties of Religious Experience* (New York: Modern Library, 1929), p. 359.
19. Ibid.
20. Ibid.
21. Ibid.
22. Herzog, *Justice Church*, p. 80.

Chapter 5. Breakthrough Step Four: Vision

1. Frederick Engels, "On the History of Early Christianity," in Karl Marx and Frederick Engels, *On Religion* (New York: Schocken Books, 1964), p. 318.
2. Interview with Frances Roots Hadden, Mackinac Island, Michigan, 20 August 1975.
3. Helen Foster Snow, *My China Years: A Memoir* (New York: William Morrow, 1984), and *Inside Red China* (1st ed. 1939; New York: Da Capo Press, 1974).
4. Edgar Snow, *Red Star over China* (1st U.S. ed. 1938; rev. ed. New York: Grove Press, 1968).
5. Pierre Teilhard de Chardin, *Building the Earth* (Denville, NJ: Dimension Books, 1965), p. 54.
6. R. C. Zaehner, *Concordant Discord* (Oxford: Clarendon Press, 1970), p. 403.
7. "St. Teresa's Bookmark," in Henry Wadsworth Longfellow, *The Complete Poetical Works* (Cambridge Edition, Houghton, Mifflin and Co., 1893), p. 597.
8. Zaehner, *Concordant Discord*, p. 374.
9. James O'Halloran, *Living Cells: Developing Small Christian Community*, rev. ed. (Maryknoll, NY: Orbis Books, 1984), and Leonardo Boff, *Ecclesiogenesis: Base Communities Reinventing the Church* (Maryknoll, NY: Orbis, 1986).

10. *Miami Herald*, 4 May 1986.

CHAPTER 6. BREAKTHROUGH STEP FIVE: THE TURNING POINT

1. St. John of the Cross, *The Dark Night of the Soul*, in *The Complete Works of St. John of the Cross*, trans. from the critical ed. of P. Silverio de Santa Teresa, C.D., and edited by E. Allison Peers, vol. 1, 3rd ed. rev. (Westminster, Md.: Newman Bookshop, 1946), pp. 409, 410.

2. Daniel Berrigan, S.J., lecture, St. Vincent de Paul Seminary, Boynton Beach, Florida, 2 February 1985.

3. Robert J. Lifton, *The Broken Connection* (New York: Simon & Schuster, 1979), chaps. 19 and 20.

4. Erich Fromm, *The Art of Loving* (New York: Harper/Colophon, 1956), p. 104.

5. R. C. Zaehner, *Concordant Discord* (Oxford: Clarendon Press, 1970), p. 395.

6. Fyodor Dostoyevsky, *The Brothers Karamazov*, trans. Constance Garnett (New York: Modern Library, n.d.), p. 270.

7. Frederick Herzog, *Justice Church* (Maryknoll, NY: Orbis Books, 1980), p. 76.

8. Dorothee Soelle, *The Strength of the Weak*, trans. Robert and Rita Kimber (Philadelphia: Westminster Press, 1984), p. 28.

9. Leszek Kolkowski, *Presentness of Myth*, quoted in Soelle, *The Strength of the Weak*, p. 24.

10. Kolkowski, ibid., p. 25.

11. Catholic Committee on Appalachia, "This Land Is Home to Me: A Pastoral Letter on Powerlessness in Appalachia by the Catholic Bishops of the Region," 1 February 1975, cited from *Renewing the Earth*, ed. David J. O'Brien and Thomas A. Shannon (New York: Doubleday/Image Books, 1977), pp. 480–81.

12. Ibid., p. 485.

13. Leo Tolstoy, *The Kingdom of God and Peace Essays*, trans. Aylmer Maude (New York: Oxford University Press, 1960).

14. "This Land Is Home to Me," in *Renewing the Earth*, pp. 488–89.

15. Vicki Kemper, "Poor and Getting Poorer," *Sojourners*, March 1986, p. 15.

16. Gregory Baum, "Ethical Reflections on the Economic Crisis," *The National Catholic Reporter*, 11 March 1983.

17. Gustavo Gutierrez, quoted in Richard Dieter, "The Impact of Liberation Theology," in *Set My People Free: Liberation Theology in Practice* (Hyattsville, MD: Quixote Center, 1986).

CHAPTER 7. BREAKTHROUGH STEP SIX: SURRENDER

1. Susan B. Anthony, *Survival Kit* (New York: New American Library, 1972), p. 62.
2. Evelyn Underhill, *Man and the Supernatural* (New York: E. P. Dutton, 1931), p. 217.
3. J. P. de Caussade, S.J., *Self-Abandonment to Divine Providence*, trans. Algar Thorold (Springfield, IL: Templegate, 1961).
4. R. C. Zaehner, *Concordant Discord* (Oxford: Clarendon Press, 1970), p. 395.
5. Martin Luther King, Jr., "Who Speaks for the South," *Liberation* 1, March 1958, quoted in *Testament of Hope: The Essential Writings of Martin Luther King, Jr.*, ed. James Melvin Washington (New York: Harper & Row, 1986), pp. 91–92.
6. Martin Luther King, Jr., "Pilgrimage to Nonviolence," *Christian Century* 77 (13 April 1960), quoted in *Testament of Hope*, pp. 91–92.
7. Ibid.
8. *Testament of Hope*, p. xxi.
9. Francine du Plessix Gray, *Divine Disobedience* (New York: Vintage Books, 1970), pp. 162–63.
10. Thomas H. Stahel, S.J., interview with John T. Ryan, S.J., and Joseph P. Parkes, S.J. in "Witness to a Revolution," *America*, 12 April 1986, pp. 297–302.
11. Ibid.
12. Ibid.
13. Ibid.
14. Ibid.
15. Quoted in Michael Nagler, "Meditation and the Challenge of Peace," *Pax Christi*, March 1986, pp. 11–13.
16. Evelyn Underhill, *The Life of the Spirit and the Life of Today* (London: Methuen & Co., 1922), pp. 215–16.
17. Evelyn Underhill, *The Church and War* (Anglican Pacifist Fellowship, n.d.), quoted in Charles Williams, ed., *The Letters of Evelyn Underhill* (London: Longman, Green & Co., 1945), p. 42.

18. Ibid., p. 41.
19. Underhill, *Man and the Supernatural*, p. 217.
20. Interviews with Rick Thomas, S.J., at charismatic conference, Saint Mary's College, Notre Dame, Indiana, July 1973.
21. Tertullian, *Apologeticum* 39, quoted in John Bartlett, *Familiar Quotations*, 12th ed., rev. and enl. (Boston: Little, Brown & Co., 1951), p. 1127.

CHAPTER 8. BREAKTHROUGH STEP SEVEN: UNION

1. Robert J. Lifton, *The Broken Connection* (New York: Simon & Schuster, 1979), p. 24.
2. Dorothee Soelle, "Mysticism-Liberation-Feminism," in *The Strength of the Weak* (Philadelphia: Westminster Press, 1984), p. 86.
3. Robert Stone, *A Flag for Sunrise* (New York: Ballantine Books, 1982), p. 416.
4. Henri Nouwen, *The Wounded Healer* (New York: Doubleday, 1979), p. 18.
5. Ibid., 17.
6. Ibid., p. 20.
7. Ibid.
8. Soelle, *The Strength of the Weak*, p. 89.
9. R. C. Zaehner, "Which God Is Dead?" in *The City Within the Heart* (New York: Crossroad, 1981), p. 7.
10. Walker Percy, *Lost in the Cosmos: The Last Self-Help Book* (New York: Farrar, Straus & Giroux, 1983), p. 114.
11. Soelle, *The Strength of the Weak*, pp. 87–88.
12. Evelyn Underhill, *Man and the Supernatural* (New York: E.P. Dutton, 1931), p. 217.
13. Ibid., pp. 217–18.
14. Gustavo Gutierrez, *A Theology of Liberation* (Maryknoll, NY: Orbis Books, 1973), p. 153.
15. Soelle, *The Strength of the Weak*, p. 80.
16. Ibid., pp. 81–82.

CHAPTER 9. TESTAMENT

1. Evelyn Underhill, *Man and the Supernatural*, p. 217.